Claus Møller

MY LIFE TREE

A different book about personal development

Published by:
TMI A/S

Translated by:
Barbara Berger

Illustrations:
Steffen Bue

Congratulations!

You now have in your hands a very special book.
One that is not finished – because YOU are going to
finish it!
It is going to be about you, your life, and the wealth
of opportunities you have.
You alone will determine the important parts of the
story because you control your own development.
You decide for yourself what your life goals are.

The first step on your road to becoming the
author of the book about your own life is to draw a
picture of yourself on page 5.

Draw it so it expresses who you would like to be,
in whatever style you like – simple, intricate, serious or funny.

If you would rather use a photograph of yourself,
choose one that you really like.

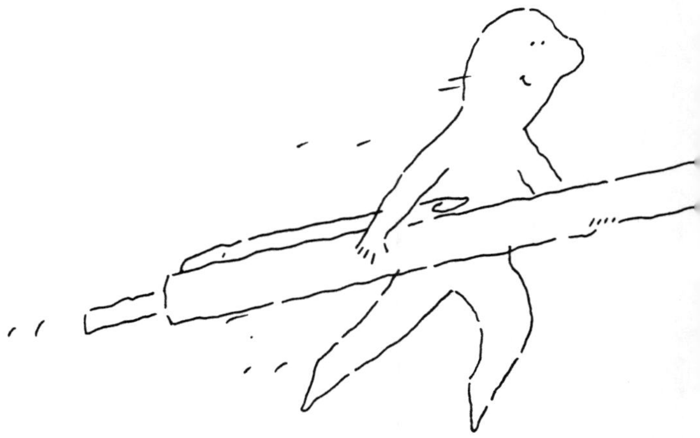

MY LIFE TREE

A Book About My Life

_____

By (Write your own name)

_____

Main character (Write your own name)

_____

_____

Supporting characters (List the other people in your life)

Table of contents

Acknowledgements

I would like to express my gratitude to the people who helped make this book a reality:

Editor *Paul Hegedahl*, B.Com., who contributed preliminary studies and material from *Putting People First*, a book we wrote together.

Professor *David Ingvar*, M.H., Ph.D., who gave significant advice and counsel for the section about "Time".

Dr. *Janelle Barlow*, Ph. D., who contributed ideas and material for the section about "Stress".

Viveca Møller, M.Sc. (psychology), who contributed inspiration, preliminary psychological studies, and ormulation. She also co-ordinated the creative presentation of the book.

Jan Løve, M.Sc (psychology), who contributed inspiration, preliminary psychological studies and formulation.

Lisbjerg, who gave both inspiration and constructive criticism.

Jytte Johansen and *Fritz Larsen*, B.Com., who were in charge of production and graphic design.

Lis Touborg, who has been an inspiring sparring-partner in the formulation of the entire book.

Claus Møller

Introduction

Dear Reader!

This book is about personal development.

When you read it, you might feel that it is about plain ordinary common sense; about what our mothers taught us; about what we all know, deep down inside.

The book is about something so simple yet so complicated as getting on in the world, something so superficial, yet essential as feeling good about yourself and other people.

It is about "something" we often expect to manage without any trouble, without ever having systematically learned anything about it.

I wrote this book because I feel there is a great need to know more about the topics in it, and because I, myself, have a great need for the ideas it contains. That is why it is perhaps primarily written to myself.

It can be regarded as a reference book in personal development. It provides help and inspiration to do some of the things which are part of creating a good life.

The book is based on events in my life, on my own personal experiences, and not least of all, on my many mistakes.

Even after years of practice, I still make some of the same mistakes, and new ones surface all the time. Now, however, I usually know what is wrong, so I have become better at getting something positive out of a negative situation.

When I tell other people how foolishly I have behaved, I often notice them smiling in relief. Nothing is more wonderful than hearing that others make the same blunders one has made oneself!

The difference between tragedy and comedy is in fact a question of who events happen to. Tragedy is when something unpleasant happens to me. Comedy is when the same thing happens to you! You will probably nod in recognition at many of the "comedies" and "tragedies" described in this book.

The book is useful for any individual who wants to improve him or herself. In addition, it can be a valuable aid for people who wish to function better together: husbands and wives, partners, parents and children, managers and employees.

Personal development is a topic which greatly interests companies and organisations because they realise that it is a prerequisite for the development of the entire company.

The opportunity for personal development determines whether a company can attract and retain capable employees, and create an environment where everyone is motivated to do their best.

I wish you a good life.

Claus Møller

1. My time is my life

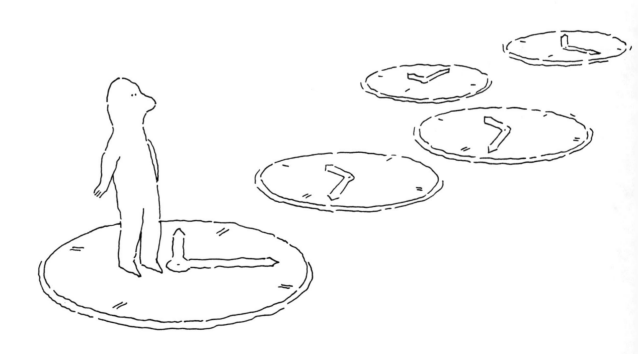

What is time?

Time is the most valuable and important resource you have, and it is up to you to use this resource fully. Your life can be regarded as the sum total of the time you have at your disposal.

Time is also the *most limited* resource you have: The only one you cannot obtain more of. You cannot buy more time, but you can *use* the time you have in the best possible way.

Time is divided into periods such as days, weeks, months, years, or into mornings, evenings and weekends.

Time is divided into work-days, leisure time, school-time, recess, breaks, waiting time, travel time, sick leave, lunch-time, dinner-time, and time to sleep.

Time is also childhood, youth, adulthood and old age.

Time passes relentlessly in a fixed rhythm: 60 seconds per minute, 60 minutes per hour, 24 hours a day.

Time passed never returns. That is why it should be against the law to steal it from others. You must create respect for your own time – and also for that of other people.

Time cannot be understood purely in a quantitative manner: It is also a question of quality. Time can pass quickly or slowly. Depending on the circumstances, people experience time differently. Sometimes it feels as if time goes by rapidly: when you feel good, when you are doing something interesting, when you are busy, or about to be late, or when something unpleasant is about to happen. Time goes by slowly when you are bored, uncommitted, or when you are waiting for something to happen which you have been looking forward to for a long time.

Time is the most democratic resource in the world. Everyday, you and everyone else has all the time there is – 24 hours – at your command. Every day, every week, every month, every year, we all have the same amount of time at our disposal, but how we make use of it varies greatly. Time is life; it can be utilised well or wasted.

By acquiring skills and developing your faculties, you can utilise your time more fully – and thus make your life more rewarding.

Many people desire eternal life
without knowing
how to get through the weekend.

A thought-provoking experience

One day I went to the supermarket to shop for the week-end. While I was putting the groceries into the boot of my car, I suddenly felt a hand on my shoulder. When I turned around, I found myself looking into a very familiar face. It was my old friend and fellow student, Peter Miller, looking the same as ever. He had recognised me right away, and said, with a big grin on his face, "You are looking just the same, old chap; but you are a little plumper!"

His voice, facial expression and laughter were just as they used to be. We had a good talk about old times and about our school days, which we both agreed were unforgettable.

After I said goodbye to Peter, I began thinking about life. Meeting him brought back a lot of wonderful memories, and some of the events we talked about seemed as real to me as if they had happened just a few years before.

But these events did not happen just a few years ago. They took place 23 years ago ...

Think how fast those 23 years went by.

I thought of adding 23 years to my present age which made me feel really odd. This simple piece of arithmetic put me well past the age of retirement; and I thought, "I certainly hope the next 23 years don't go by so fast".

The older one becomes, the faster time seems to pass by. The time between one New Year's Eve and the next becomes shorter and shorter. Many retired people feel as though the last 20 years have passed as quickly as 5 years of their childhood because on an emotional level, the period between 45 and 65 feels about as long as that from 10 to 15.

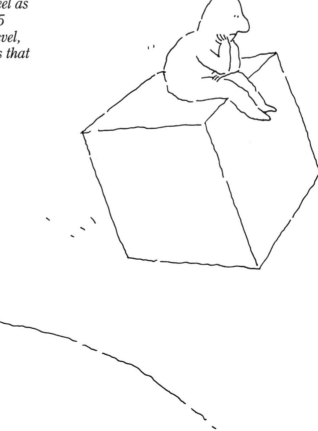

EXERCISE 1: How fast does my time fly?

Think back 5 years

Sit down in a comfortable chair and think back 5 years.
Ask yourself these questions:

- How old was I?

- Where did I live?

- Was I living with someone?

- Did I have children?

- How old were they?

- How did I use my leisure time – In the morning? In the evening? At weekends?

- Where did I work?

- What position did I have?

- Which skills did I have then; and have I developed them since?

- What types of technology were used in my company?

- Which technical aids did we use at home? Have we acquired new ones since then?

   Did the last 5 years go by quickly, or did they pass slowly?
   You will probably feel that they went by quickly – and at the same time, that it was long, long ago, because so much has happened since then.

Think ahead 20 years

Imagine that you are 20 years older.
   Add 20 years to your present age.
   How old would you be?
   With this in mind, you probably cannot imagine anything more important than making the most of the time ahead. Try to imagine that in 5 years from now, you are 20 years older.

My relationship to time

Time exists as a constant element in our thoughts and our minds.

Consciously or unconsciously, our thoughts revolve around time, as we try to place each action or situation in relation to it.

We continuously seek the answers to a series of questions about time – from the most simple, to the most complex:

- What time is it?
- Is there an eternal life?

Between these extremes, we ask questions like:

- How much time should I spend on my private life?
- How much time should I spend working?
- How much time should I spend with my family and friends?
- How much time should I spend on myself?
- What is most important? I can't do everything.
- How can I make the time go by more quickly?
- Where will I find time to do it?
- How can I make my time more worthwhile?
- How can I avoid becoming stressed by the pressures of time?
- What do I want to get out of life before I die?
- When should I start a family?
- How long can I stay in good health?
- How much time do I have left to live?
- Why wasn't he/she permitted to live longer?
- When will the children move away from home?
- When will I get a new job?
- When will I be promoted?
- How long do we have to wait for an answer?
- Why don't people meet their deadlines?
- How much time should I use on my own development?
- When will there be peace?
- When will others learn to understand . . . ?
- When will pollution stop?
- When will the next generation of EDP equipment appear?
- How long will the present government stay in office?

There are probably no definitive answers to these questions.

They are, however, eternally relevant, and the whole of life can be regarded as a search for answers.

Time attracts our thoughts with a magnetic force. Most conversations contain aspects of time; and it is difficult to maintain communication without touching upon our relationship to time:
"Where is Ann?" "She's on vacation!"
We are almost obliged to say:
"When is she coming back?"

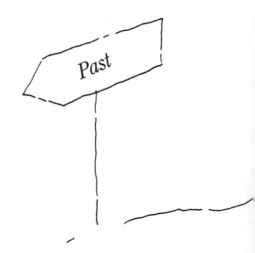

Past - Present - Future

Everyone consciously experiences life as a flow of events moving from that which was, through the present, towards that which will be.

The past exists in our memory. The present exists in our minds; and the future exists in our visions, according to Saint Augustine.

Life can be regarded as a time continuum along which you are constantly moving, from the day you were born until the day you die.

It is vitally important to make the most of time, and thus of life, while that fleeting moment – the present – passes by.

There is no dress rehearsal for life.
You only get one chance to live – now!

The meaning of the present

Everyone wants to live a good life. But this doesn't happen all by itself. We ourselves are responsible for creating it.

The only part of our life we can do something about is *the present.*

A good life is one with many good NOWs.

Part of being happy is the ability to live in the NOW and enjoy it.

Many people imagine that happiness is waiting somewhere out in the future. It can only be achieved when a new situation is created, when new possessions are acquired, or when present conditions change drastically.

Gradually, as life moves on, and we grow older and more experienced, we realise that happiness doesn't just exist in the future. Little by little, we find out that the past also held many good NOWs. At the time, they were just difficult to see. Once, for example, we thought that happiness was leaving school. Later we understand that happiness is enjoying each and every school day to the fullest.

The more experience we gain, the more we realise that maybe happiness is not so much reaching a goal as enjoying every moment – *the present* – on our way towards it.

Stop

...as often as possible during the day, week, month and year and say to yourself: "What can I do – right here and now – to make the most of the present situation?" Then do it! Because this will maximise the number of times you feel good right now which must be the greatest possible happiness!

Once in a while, stop and ask yourself: "Is what I'm doing right now, the best possible use of my time? Does it help create a better life for myself and for others, now and in the future? Or am I using my time in the wrong way – going in the wrong direction?"

Living in the moment

To live in the moment's a well-worn routine
that most of the world has perfected;
for some, it's the moment that's already been,
for others, – the one that's expected.

Yet no sort of magic can kindle anew
a past that is over forever,
nor summon the future before it is due:
our moment is now – or it's never.

So brief is the moment in which we may live,
and future or past it isn't.
Whoever would know of what life has to give
must gratefully welcome the present.

Piet Hein

I am going to enjoy the present – right now!

Guidelines for living in the present

Our experience of the NOW creates an image of our life situation, at this very moment.

The mind compares each moment with the one which just passed and with the one we believe is coming. The present is compared to the past and related to the future as we see it.

Our actions are shaped partially by what we have done and partially by what we expect of the future. When our actions are in harmony with our past experiences and future expectations, we thrive, feel good and are happy.

Sometimes we feel that *the present* is "wrong" in one way or another. It is not consistent with our images from the past and does not reflect the future we expect. Such a disparity fills us with distaste, uneasiness, and perhaps anxiety. In this way, tension, depression and pessimism can arise, and even cause a variety of physical as well as mental problems.

You can actively work to experience every moment in time as a good NOW. This demands working on 3 fronts:

1. Your thoughts about the past.
2. Your thoughts about the future.
3. Your control of *the present.*

To enjoy *the present,* it is important not to focus too much on negative pictures from the past, but try leafing through yesterday's positive images instead.

It is just as important that you think positively about your future – that you look forward to it. And that you fight any anxiety for the unknown which lies ahead.

Finally, it is vitally important for your ability to enjoy *the present,* that you maintain control of your situation by organising and creating an overview of the next 24 hours.

My thoughts about the past

Our minds contain a storehouse of information about our past in the form of knowledge and skills, experiences and memories.

The mind constantly chooses the most significant information from the stream of impressions which catches our attention. This holds true for impressions of ourselves, our surroundings, and the groups we belong to. The mind chooses the information it considers important, works it into our memories, and keeps it there.

This storehouse is like an enormous archive from which we consciously and unconsciously draw the pictures that become a part of our overall view of the *present.*

To enjoy *the present,* it is important not to let mistakes from the past – unwise decisions, bad luck, miscalculations, fiascos and thwarted expectations – cast their shadow upon it.

Too many people ruin *the present* by regretting things which happened in the past, things they cannot do anything about anyway.

When you discover that you have made a mistake, or made the wrong decision, don't waste your time regretting it – rejoice in the fact that you have become that much wiser. With your new experience, you should be able to avoid landing in the same situation in the future.

You can work consciously to make the most out of the present by summoning forth the most suitable and positive pictures from your past.

My thoughts about the future

A large part of our mental activity is occupied with the future. The mind is always trying to create pictures of the future along with an accompanying set of expectations.

We imagine different types of life goals and patterns of behaviour, and we create small programmes in our minds about the future. The purpose of these programmes is that they are kept in readiness, and that they help lead us towards the goals we have defined and are consciously or subconsciously trying to reach. We imagine how the future is going to be – at its best and at its worst; and we prepare alternative plans to deal with whatever it might bring.

Thoughts about the future occupy a large part of our consciousness and greatly influence the way we experience *the present. The present* turns out better when we think positively and constructively about the future.

Many people are uncertain about the future – some even fear it; and anxiety about the future can fill *the present* with frustration, worry, negative fantasies, and the inability to act. Some people have a hard time deciding if they should stay in their present position or find another one.

Some find it difficult to decide if they should continue their relationship or end it.

Some people are so unsure about the future that they hardly dare decide whether to have coffee or tea with their lunch!

Many continually postpone decisions and hope others will make them for them. Perhaps, they do so out of fear that they will regret it if they make unwise decisions.

You can work consciously to create positive expectations about the future and to establish the belief that you can greatly influence your future in a positive direction.

You can also learn to make better decisions – and live with them.

When you are young, you probably don't worry so much about the future. In most cases, there is a lot of future out there, so it should be possible to get something out of it.

Gradually, as you get older, the future seems less vast than it once was, and you may feel your opportunities are more limited.

You must work at having visions – no matter what your age.

Controlling the present

To enjoy *the present,* you must be able to control it; and you can only do so if you focus on it. Many people are not capable of enjoying *the present* because their thoughts about it keep getting side-tracked.

Their ability to concentrate can be weakened by regrets about the past, and by fear and uncertainty concerning the future.

One major cause of this is simply a lack of overview, leading to confusion, unfinished tasks and loose ends.

Having a good overview of the next 24 hours provides many advantages. If you:

- have a plan for the next few days
- know which larger tasks you must complete
- know which smaller chores you must remember
- know who to write or call
- know which decisions you must make and
- are reasonably organised

you:

- increase your energy
- decrease your level of stress
- improve your ability to concentrate
- raise the quality of your performance
- enhance your capacity and
- gain more control over *the present*

Overview and organisation do not mean that you lose spontaneity and creativity.

On the contrary.

With more strength, energy, and an increased capacity for concentration, you can become even more spontaneous and creative.

You also gain a new perspective on life. It is easier to distinguish the essential from the non-essential, and to focus on what matters: Living in *the present* – and enjoying it.

The only part of your life
you can do something about
is
the present

A good life is a life
with many good NOWs

Part of being happy is
the ability to
live in the NOW
– and enjoy it

Enjoy the present
Don't feel guilty about the past
Don't be afraid of the future
Take control of the present

Learn to notice and enjoy
even the tiniest thing

EXERCISE 2: My time axis

Place an × on the continuum
below at the point you feel
you have reached in your life.

|—————————————————|—————————————————|
Birth   Midway   Death

Now look at the position of your ×.
Take a moment to reflect a little about life.

Ask yourself these questions:	Your comments:
Why did I place my × where I did?	
What have I got out of my past?	
What do I wish to achieve in the future?	
Am I going in the right direction? Or should I make some changes in my life?	

Ask yourself these questions:	Your comments:
Can I concentrate on the NOW?	
Can I enjoy the NOW?	
Can I refrain from regretting the past?	
Do I look forward to the future?	
Can I make decisions – and live with them?	
Have I learned to regard my mistakes as valuable experiences?	
How much of my life do I live in the past?	
How much of my life do I live in the future?	
How much of my life do I live in the NOW?	

2. How do I look at life?
Pearls and the present

Imagine that every instant gives you the opportunity
to create a bright spot in your life, a satisfying *moment,* a rich and eventful NOW. In short, a "pearl".

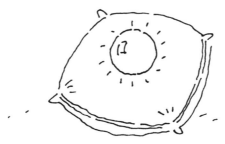

You can see life as a string of pearls.

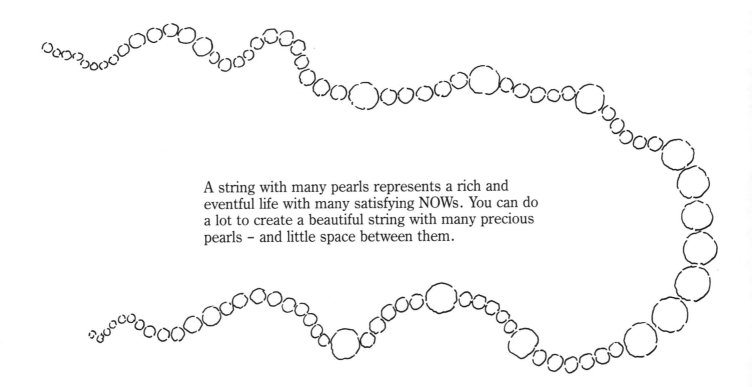

A string with many pearls represents a rich and
eventful life with many satisfying NOWs. You can do
a lot to create a beautiful string with many precious
pearls – and little space between them.

A string with a few, small pearls represents a less
interesting life with few high spots. Don't cheat
yourself. Don't collect "fake" pearls.

*You have the chance to create pearls –
every morning and evening, every day, weekend and holiday.*

You carry around 3 types of images or "pictures",
positive, negative and neutral, of the experiences
in your life; and how you perceive *the present* is
determined to an extent by the image you decide to
create.

Every person is their own "creator".

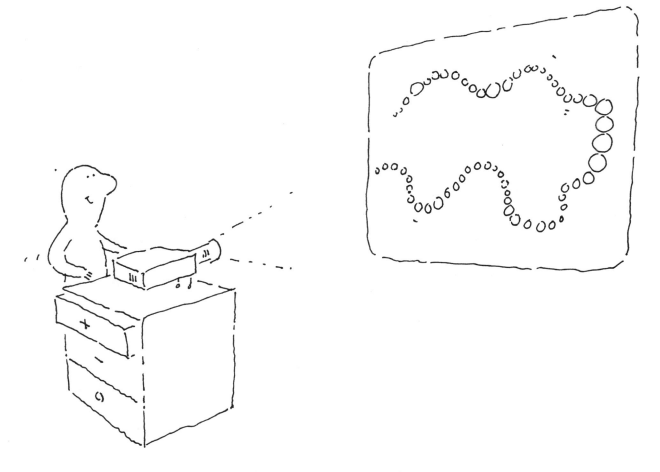

At every moment in time, you register an image
which you place in an archive and which is crucial to
how you experience *the present*.

You can select from the archive experiences, feelings and perceptions which are positive, negative or
neutral – and when you create new images, you decide which they are going to be.

*You decide whether you want to be a pearl-crusher
or a pearl-fisher – or if you want to be "pearl-blind".*

Pearl-crusher

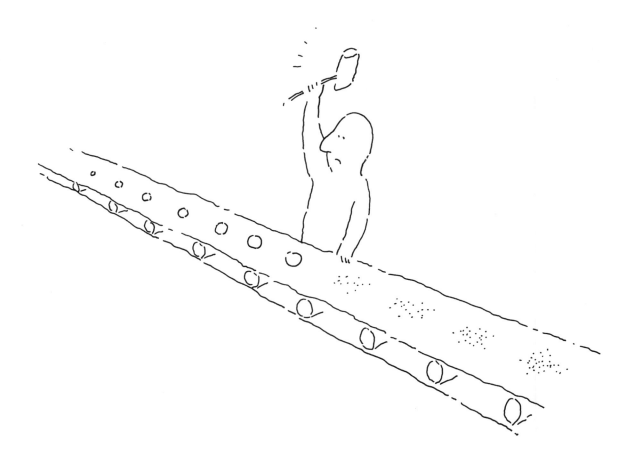

Some people have a special talent for destroying the NOW – for crushing pearls. You could call these people *pearl-crushers*. Most of the time, they retrieve negative pictures from their archive.

It doesn't take much for these people to decide to ruin the NOW – for themselves and for everyone else around.

Pearl-fisher

Some people have a special talent for making the most of the NOW – for creating pearls. We can call these people *pearl-fishers*. Most of the time, they retrieve pictures from their positive archive.

The pearl-fisher understands that it's not hard to find, catch, keep and enjoy pearls if one is creative and looks at the NOW with positive eyes. Pearl-fishers find pearls both for themselves and for others.

Examples of pearl-crushers and pearl-fishers

A pearl-crusher goes to a dinner party

*At a dinner party, my partner is involved in intense conversation with the person seated next to him or her. This person is of the opposite sex – and is not making the slightest effort to hide it. From where I'm sitting, it doesn't seem as though my partner minds continuing the exchange, and seems to be thinking, "It's been a long time since someone devoured **me** with their eyes like this".*

I certainly hope my partner is all talked out when we get home because we aren't going to have much to talk about in the next few days!

A pearl-fisher goes to a dinner party

At a dinner party, my partner is involved in intense conversation with the person seated next to him or her. This person is of the opposite sex – and is not making the slightest effort to hide it. It's wonderful to see my partner in good company and enjoying the evening. I'm sure we're going to have a good time; and I'm really looking forward to meeting this new, exciting person.

It turns out that the person my partner was talking so intensely to is an author. Since the party, we've met several times, and this has added a whole new dimension to our lives.

Which of these two are you most like
when you go to a dinner party?

A pearl-crusher goes to a seminar

After much thought, I decided to participate in a seminar on personal development. I have always been very sceptical about programmes such as this – even though I've never participated in one.

I didn't expect much from the seminar – and I can assure you that the organisers did everything possible to live up to my expectations. It was almost impossible to find a parking place, and my name was spelt wrongly on my name tag. There wasn't enough tea during the first break, and we weren't allowed to smoke in the room.

I was so irritated about all this that I didn't get very much out of the first half of the programme. When I finally got over my irritation, I began to realise that the seminar was actually rather good. But then again – considering the cost – it should be!

*Now I just regret that my boss didn't attend. Some of my colleagues should also have participated. **They** could really have learned something! I will be sure to tell them when I see them.*

A pearl-fisher goes to a seminar

Since the whole world is in the process of development, I too must develop myself personally, and decided to attend a seminar on the subject. I was really looking forward to this event and to being with other people who also wish to improve themselves.

There was so much interest in the programme, that it was difficult to find a parking place; so I parked a short distance from the conference centre. This gave me the chance to take a pleasant walk through the beautiful grounds surrounding the centre.

The seminar was about change. It was exciting. The organisers had even tried to change my name by spelling it in a completely new way on the name tag. I met many interesting people and even became rather popular when I managed to rustle up some extra tea during the break.

I learned a lot and defined those areas I need to work on to improve myself. I have already changed in some ways, which both my boss and my colleagues have noticed: so now they too want to attend the programme.

Which of the two are you most like
when you go to a seminar?

A pearl-crusher on the road

I'm sitting in my car, a little late, again. I didn't really have time to eat breakfast, so I "inhaled" it.

Oh no - why are all those cars stopped up ahead? That's just what I need: road works ahead!

I decide to breathe rapidly and pump adrenaline into my blood. Why don't those idiots move? Who in the world would decide to do road work during the day, and in the middle of the rush hour? We pay enough tax as it is.

What now? No, this is too much: someone is trying to pass the whole queue on the hard shoulder. Just wait until I catch him up! The police are never around when you need them.

Now someone else is doing it – and another – and another. Well, why not? You are seldom rewarded for following the rules. I am going to overtake, too! That went just fine. Everything is moving along much faster now. Just think about all those cowards who are still sitting in the queue.

What now? A car with flashing lights? A man in uniform! Why is he waving me to the side? Don't the police have anything better to do?

A pearl-fisher on the road

I am sitting in my car, feeling relaxed after a nice breakfast with my family. I enjoy driving to work every morning. It gives me a chance to reflect a little about life.

They seem to have started working on the road today, so maybe I will be a little late for work. Oh well, it can't pay to get upset about it. I suppose I had better leave home a little earlier tomorrow. Now I might just as well use this delay profitably. It's a good thing I have my "French for Beginners" tape and my favourite music in the car. Sometimes it's really nice not to be interrupted by the telephone.

Which of the two are you most like
when you are on the road?

A pearl-crusher goes on holiday

I work hard all year long and really look forward to a well-earned annual holiday.

One year, we spent our holiday in a cottage in England. I'll never do that again. It rained constantly, all day long, the whole time, so we had to sit inside and wait for the sun to come out. People get on each other's nerves when they are cooped up, without really having anything to do – and all because of the weather!

Another year, we went to Greece. I'll never do that again either. It was unbearably warm, and I got sunburnt on the very first day. I spent a fortune on suntan lotions and sunglasses. I felt best when I could sit inside with a cold drink and read a book. However, there wasn't much chance of that, because my nagging children were constantly trying to drag me outside to one of the many activities the locals were trying to palm off on the tourists.

Finally, we were on a river cruise one year in France. Apart from the many locks, we had a good time. It's just a shame these holidays are so short because by the time you start to relax, you've got to go to work again. I spent the first week of holiday trying to unwind, and the last week thinking about all the things that were probably piling up at work, just waiting for me.

I really don't know if I feel like going on holiday any more.

A pearl-fisher goes on holiday

I work hard all year round and really look forward to a well-earned annual holiday.

One year we spent our holiday in a cottage in England. The weather was more suitable to indoor activities than outdoor activities, so we bought sturdy rain gear for the whole family which was actually cheaper than buying it back home. The weather gave us an unusual chance to be together, talk a lot and do things together indoors. We read and listened to music. We went for walks in the fresh air, and met many of the local inhabitants who had to go out in the rain. England is a wonderful country.

Another year, we went to Greece, and we were very lucky with the weather. The sun shone brightly from a cloudless sky. I got a little sunburnt on the first day, but it gave me the chance to sit indoors the next day and enjoy a cold beer while the rest of the family enjoyed themselves with all sorts of outdoor activities. The local taverns had wonderful food and music, and the resort offered both relaxing entertainment and cultural sights. Greece is a wonderful country.

One year we went cruising on a river in France. It was marvellous. It was so relaxing. Just sailing the barge demanded so much concentration that we completely forgot about our jobs. Before going on holiday, I managed to prepare for the project I was supposed to be working on after the holiday, so I didn't leave too many loose ends behind. That certainly helped me enjoy every day of our two weeks completely. France is a wonderful country.

Which of the two are you most like
when you are on holiday?

EXERCISE 3: When I was a pearl-crusher

List below a few situations, from both your personal and professional life, when you have acted like a pearl-crusher. *Examples:* When my son spilt chocolate milk on our new rug; when some odious person ruined the aerial on my car; when my colleague, who is not especially bright, got promoted; when the price of oil went up.

Times when I was a pearl-crusher:

In the future, try to be aware of situations which bring out the pearl-crusher in you. Is there a special pattern to your behaviour? Ask yourself: How often am I a pearl-crusher? What do I get out of being a pearl-crusher? How could I have become a pearl-fisher instead in the same situation?

EXERCISE 4: When I was a pearl-fisher

List a few situations, from both your personal and professional life, when you have acted like a pearl-fisher. *Examples:* When the guests arrived late for our dinner party; when I started talking to the person sitting next to me on the plane; when my children picked the first rose of the year – without the stem; when our garden party was rained out.

Times when I was a pearl-fisher:

In the future, try to be even more aware of situations which encourage the pearl-fisher in you.
Make finding pearls in ordinary, everyday situations a habit. In this way, you are creating a rich and eventful life.

Is your life "a dance on pearls"?

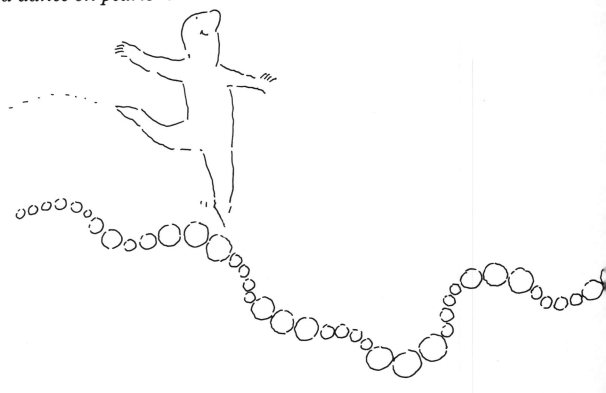

...or is it difficult for you to keep your balance on your string of pearls?

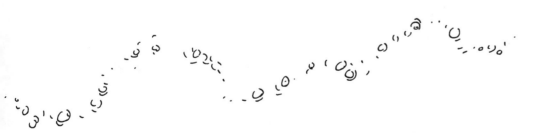

*Your outlook on life – your attitude towards yourself and your surroundings
– determines whether you become a pearl-crusher or a pearl-fisher.*

3. My personal development

– my life tree

This whole book is about *your* development and the ways in which you change and grow.

A tree can be regarded as a symbol for growth and the roots, the soil, the trunk and the crown all play a role in the tree's development.

It is up to you whether your "life tree" grows tall and majestic with a straight trunk, many branches, leaves and a beautiful crown, or if it ends up being a poor, stunted tree which creeps along the ground.

Your life tree has 4 parts:

A. The roots – your attitudes towards life
B. The soil – your surroundings
C. The trunk – your personal goals
D. The branches – your knowledge and skills

My attitudes towards life – my roots

The roots of your tree represent your attitudes towards life. Your tree has many roots, which means that you can adopt many different attitudes towards your life and personal development. Your roots can be more or less capable of absorbing nourishment, giving life, and promoting growth.

Some roots/attitudes which promote growth are: I am OK; others are OK; I am responsible for my life; I believe life is a gift; people are exciting; I'm so lucky.

Roots/attitudes which limit growth are: I am not-OK; others are not-OK; I am a victim of circumstance; life is a vale of tears; other people are so difficult.

You should work continually with your roots – your attitudes towards yourself and your surroundings – because they are so important for your personal development, well-being and effectiveness. The more you work with your roots, the healthier and stronger the network will become: your potential for growth will increase, and your life tree will stand firm in the fiercest storm, and survive for many years.

My surroundings - my soil

The growth of your tree – your development – is determined, not only by your roots/attitudes, but also by your surroundings.

The soil is the nourishment your roots receive and the environment they are planted in. It is the surroundings you find yourself in – at home and at work.

There is one particular root which largely determines your growth, effectiveness and well-being. That root is your self-esteem or "OK feeling"; and if your surroundings contribute to this, you will function well and grow. If you are satisfied with yourself, you will bubble with high spirits, and have the extra energy needed to be there for others and to manage difficult situations. It is quite correct when people say you have to love yourself in order to have the capacity to "be" something for others.

Recognition is the best nourishment for your "OK feeling" and thus for your life tree: it is just as important for people as sunshine is for trees and other plants.

Everyone is responsible for his or her own growth. However, most people are to a large extent dependent upon the recognition of others though some are so tough that they can feel good about themselves without it. You can work consciously with your "OK feeling" by recognising and appreciating yourself which is, in fact, imperative for being able to accept the recognition and appreciation of others.

Remember that each person has the power to fertilise or destroy the soil which nourishes other people's life trees.

Companies and organisations should learn to create the most fertile soil possible for their employees' life trees. In this way, they ensure the growth of a whole forest, which becomes an appealing place for all employees, business associates and others who are important to the growth of the entire company. Managers should learn to promote the growth of their employees. Parents, too, should learn to give their children's life trees the best possible conditions for growth.

It is important that you learn to establish and maintain your own self-esteem and to strengthen the "OK feelings" of the people in your life.

My personal goals - my trunk

Constantly defining your overall personal and professional goals – and the experience of reaching them – plays a central role in your life. Achieving goals is crucial to your development, effectiveness and sense of well-being.

The trunk of the tree represents the backbone of your life – your life goals. The feeling of working towards a goal and the experience of achieving it, together make your life worth living. When you have clearly-defined life goals, visions, and faith in the future, your life is more meaningful and you are better able to live in the present.

My knowledge and skills - my branches

In order to function and develop, you need a number of fundamental qualities and skills. You must continually plan, set priorities, create overview, make decisions, understand, learn, remember, communicate, solve problems, ensure quality and delegate. Furthermore, you need to exercise self-discipline, be creative and flexible, display tolerance, learn to live with stress, and keep your knowledge and attitudes up-to-date.

The crown of the tree – branches, twigs and leaves – is also a sign of your growth. The crown determines whether other people think that your tree is attractive, special, harmonious, and worth getting to know. The branches are your knowledge and skills; and developing these opens doors, enriches your life, and makes you a more exciting person to those around you.

The remainder of this book is built up around your life tree.

EXERCISE 5: How my life tree looks today

For each of the tree's 4 parts, both write and draw
how you experience your life tree today. How
strong and vital are your roots? How thick is your
trunk? How well-developed are your branches?
Are some of them weaker than others? What kind
of soil is your life tree growing in?

Use words, pictures, symbols and colours. If
necessary, use a bigger piece of paper.

Show your picture to your partner/friend, and
talk about it with him or her.

EXERCISE 6: How I want my life tree to look

For each of the tree's 4 parts, write and draw how you want your life tree to look.

Use words, pictures, symbols and colours. If necessary, use a bigger piece of paper.

In which ways does your actual life tree differ from your "dream tree"? Which parts of the tree do you need to work on in order to make it more closely resemble this "dream"?

Show your picture to your partner/friend, and talk about it with him or her.

4. My attitudes towards life

– my roots

This entire chapter deals with your attitudes towards life – the roots of your life tree as described in chapter 3.

Your sense of well-being, your effectiveness and your entire development are largely determined by these attitudes, i.e. the way you see yourself, and the different people, conditions and circumstances which surround you.

Your attitudes develop continually. They are formed in childhood through contact with parents, siblings, friends and teachers, and as an adult, they are influenced by family, friends, colleagues, business contacts, society, and the media – as well as by your other attitudes, which exert mutual influence.

In chapter 2, you read about the pearl-crusher and the pearl-fisher, concepts which express different attitudes towards life in TMI terminology.

In this chapter, you will delve more deeply into the concept of attitudes and into modern psychology.

As described previously, people may have different attitudes towards life:

● Winner/loser
● Positive/negative
● Committed/uncommitted
● Responsible for your own achievements/ a victim of circumstance
● Other people are OK/other people are not-OK
● I am OK/I am not-OK

Every attitude can be illustrated with the help of a scale which moves from something positive to something negative. Your behaviour, whether suitable or unsuitable, is largely determined by where you are on the attitude scale right now – though you need not remain at the same point for the rest of your life. For every attitude, you can choose to move in a positive or negative direction.

The most important attitude on the scale is:

I am OK/I am not-OK

because it rubs off on all your other attitudes and your surroundings and therefore has a crucial effect on the whole of your behaviour.

It is important to move up to the positive end of the OK attitude scale. To create the feeling – I am OK.

This is the feeling known as self-esteem.

The importance of self-esteem

Creating and maintaining self-esteem is of the utmost importance for your growth, well-being and effectiveness.

Managers' most important task is to encourage the ongoing development of *their employees' self-esteem.*

Parents' most important task is to encourage the ongoing development of *their children's self-esteem.*

Spouses' most important task is to encourage the ongoing development of *their partner's self-esteem.*

Your self-esteem is not fixed and unchanging. It is greatly influenced by your *successes* and *failures.*

You can and should work with your self-esteem all the time.

If you do not possess self-esteem, you will be unable to encourage others to have it.

How great is your self-esteem right now?

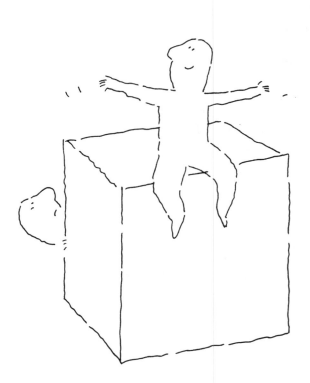

EXERCISE 7: Measure your self-esteem

How to do this exercise:

● Evaluate the statements on page 46 and 47 as objectively as possible.

● Place an × in the **Agree** column, if you agree completely with the statement.

● Place an × in the **Partially** column if you partially agree or disagree with the statement.

● Place an × in the **Disagree** column if you disagree completely with the statement.

How to score this exercise:

● Count the number of ×s in each of the 3 columns. Write the sum in the space marked **Number of ×s.**

● Multiply the number of ×s in the **Agree** column by 3. Put the result in the space provided for **Points.**

● Write the number of ×s in the **Partially** column in the space provided for **Points.**

● Do not count the number of ×s in the **Disagree** column.

● Add up the numbers in the two different Points spaces and write the sum in the space marked **Total.**

The maximum number of points is 90.

A score of more than 70 points indicates a high degree of self-esteem. In other words, you feel good about yourself and others.

If you score considerably less than 70 points, you should work on developing your self-esteem – and regard this task as an exciting challenge.

It can also be beneficial to ask others, your boss, colleagues, employees, friends and family, to score this exercise as they see you. This will probably reveal some differences that are worth working with.

to be continued

How is my self-esteem?	Agree	Partially	Disagree
1. I find it easy to accept recognition and praise without feeling embarrassed.			
2. I find it easy to make contact with other people.			
3. I reprimand others in a way that allows them to retain their self-esteem.			
4. I do not make others feel guilty.			
5. I do not need to prove that I am better than others.			
6. I am able to enjoy other people's success.			
7. I do not feel inferior to others.			
8. I focus more on other people's strengths than on their weaknesses.			
9. I believe that other people's intentions are good, until proven otherwise.			
10. My past actions seldom make me feel guilty.			
11. I fight for my own ideas and opinions.			
12. I am honest with myself.			
13. I don't feel hurt when other people have different ideas and opinions than I do.			
14. I regard most problems as exciting challenges.			
15. I do not seek gain at the expense of others.			
16. I seldom play the "martyr".			
17. I can be alone with myself – and enjoy it.			

How is my self-esteem?	Agree	Partially	Disagree
18. I don't humiliate others.			
19. I am not afraid to admit my mistakes.			
20. I trust myself and my own judgement.			
21. I seldom fear the future.			
22. I don't get upset about things I can't do anything about.			
23. I do not react inappropriately when I experience defeat or when I am disappointed.			
24. I have a great deal of self-discipline. When I decide to change a habit, I stick to the decision.			
25. I rarely envy others.			
26. I rarely feel jealous.			
27. I rarely feel bored.			
28. I am not afraid of showing my innermost feelings.			
29. I don't blame others for my problems.			
30. I find it easy to recognise and praise others.			
Number of ✕s			
Points			
Total			

Feeling OK and not-OK

Every person creates a picture in his or her brain of how their ideal life should be.

Your ideal picture includes your overall life goals and views – both material and non-material – and is composed of a series of small mosaics which depict your wishes and expectations with regard to:

- behaviour
- challenges
- achievements
- other people's opinions of you
- recognition/criticism
- experiences
- relationships with others
- social status
- right/wrong
- education
- lifestyle
- appearance

Whenever your experience of reality is close to your ideal picture, you will feel OK.

Whenever your experience of reality seems fundamentally different from your ideal, it will provoke a feeling of not-OK-ness.

The amount of self-esteem you have – your position on the OK/not-OK scale is vitally important for:

- your thoughts
- your feelings
- your appearance
- your entire behaviour

Feeling OK

When your self-esteem is high – when you feel OK – you have a series of positive experiences, and feel:

- happy
- successful
- optimistic
- free
- energetic, with a high level of performance
- courageous, in the face of new challenges
- visionary, with a belief in the future
- confident, in yourself and others
- committed
- responsible

The greater your self-esteem, the easier it will be for you to:

- be something for others
- achieve results
- inspire those around you
- give substance and meaning to your life
- live fully in the present

Feeling not-OK

When your self-esteem is low – when you do not feel OK – you have a series of negative experiences, and feel:

- inadequate
- frustrated and disappointed
- indifferent
- uncertain
- envious
- pessimistic
- uninspired
- tired, with a low level of performance
- guilty
- afraid of the future
- empty
- depressed

The lower your self-esteem, the more likely you are to:

- spoil your relationships with others
- prevent yourself from achieving results
- destroy the present and, in the process, your life

Experiencing self-esteem

The first step towards developing self-esteem is to become aware of your position on the OK scale at this very moment.

By paying attention both to your *OK* an *not-OK signals,* you can get a feeling of how much self-esteem you have.

OK signals

Some of the feelings and experiences which characterise feeling OK were described earlier. Train yourself to be aware of these and similar feelings.

The checklist below can help you identify OK signals and encourage OK behaviour.

Checklist: OK signals

People who feel OK make up their own minds and take responsibility. They:

- live in the present without guilt or fear
- perceive problems as challenges
- know their own strengths and weaknesses and know they can improve
- respect others and themselves
- are tolerant
- are flexible and adapt easily to new situations
- are not afraid to take risks
- are not afraid to go beyond ordinary limits
- enjoy new challenges
- are pleased to see change
- are genuinely pleased by other people's success
- are ready to do their best
- show initiative
- are friendly and helpful
- seldom complain
- are guided by their own opinions and convictions
- change rules, decisions and principles when it is wise to do so
- admit their mistakes without trying to justify them
- learn from their own mistakes
- accept other people's mistakes – once
- reprimand others in a way that allows them to retain their OK feeling
- don't like failure and fight to the end to avoid it
- do not categorise themselves or others
- are willing to co-operate
- set high quality standards for themselves and others
- do not make others feel guilty
- concentrate on their own success and not on other people's failures
- are able to make the most of a situation
- do not fear competition
- utilise their own abilities and skills
- can always find something good to say about others
- are not afraid to express their positive thoughts
- feel that life offers endless opportunities

Not-OK signals

Examples of feeling not-OK were described earlier. Pay attention to these and similar feelings.

The checklist below can help you identify not-OK signals and encourage you to avoid inappropriate behaviour.

Checklist: Not-OK signals

People who do not feel OK are not independent.

They follow the crowd and feel they are the victims of circumstance. They:

- live according to what they believe other people think about them
- feel that they have no influence on the course of events
- feel inadequate, unimportant and unworthy
- are afraid of challenges
- refrain from close human contact out of fear of being disappointed
- refrain from helping others – mainly because they feel their help is of no use
- are guided by rules, principles and prejudices
- often play the "martyr"
- over-administer systems and exploit the power of their positions
- are often envious
- stick to the known and become uncertain when confronted with something new
- are afraid of being alone, but find it difficult to join established groups
- often criticise themselves and others
- are afraid to express their own opinions and convictions
- often feel guilty and try to give others guilt feelings
- refrain from acting out of fear of failure and criticism
- often think of the future with apprehension
- live in the past and talk about the good old days
- seek gain at the expense of others
- stress the importance of their own efforts by downplaying the efforts of others
- don't accept others' mistakes
- justify their own mistakes
- use other people's ideas and present them as their own
- often complain
- find it difficult to acknowledge their own and others' efforts
- are malicious and gloating
- don't keep their promises
- are unable to say no
- lie to themselves and others
- withhold information
- spread rumours – talk *about* people instead of *to* them

Examples of OK reactions and not-OK reactions

Each of the situations below is followed by a typical OK reaction and typical not-OK reaction.
Read the examples through and try to imagine how you would react.

OK reaction	Not-OK reaction
You discover you paid too much in a shop. You point out the mistake and ask them to correct it.	You don't want to make a fuss and therefore say nothing.
The driver of another car intentionally annoys you in traffic. You don't let the other driver's inappropriate behaviour affect you.	You follow the "idiot" and try to exact a dreadful revenge.
A colleague criticises your work. You decide to look upon the criticism as something positive and constructive – or else ignore it.	You react emotionally and try to place the blame elsewhere.
Your partner unexpectedly changes plans and expects you to follow suit. The changes create tremendous problems for you and the people you have made arrangements with. You decide to carry out your original plans. You explain to your partner why and ask to be notified well in advance next time.	You change your plans and place yourself in an awkward position. You criticise your partner loudly while other people are around.
You are on a diet and feel wildly hungry. You resist the temptation to eat unwisely.	You devour a whole raspberry tart and feel miserable, both mentally and physically.
While out dining, you are served a well-done steak, even though you ordered medium-rare. You ask the waiter to please exchange your steak for a medium-rare one.	You eat the well-done steak because you don't want to make a fuss. You promise yourself never to set foot in that restaurant again.
While on a diet, you are invited to dinner. The hostess insists you eat a portion of a very delicious, but extremely fattening dessert she made especially for you. You decline without offending your hostess.	You eat 2 portions "very reluctantly" because you don't want to offend your hostess.

OK reaction	Not-OK reaction

A colleague asks you to come to the telephone even though you had both agreed that you were not to be disturbed for the next hour.

You tell your colleague when you can return the call and remind him or her of your agreement.	Even though you object, you allow yourself to be disturbed. You feel frustrated and your plan for the day falls apart.

You feel like telling your parents that you love them.

You get yourself together and express your feelings warmly and naturally.	You don't tell them because you are afraid that it will seem odd. You are also unsure of how your parents will react.

A colleague tries to get you to undertake an assignment, completely outside your normal sphere of work, which he or she doesn't feel like doing - even though they have the time and the necessary background, and have already agreed to do it.

You say no in a friendly way, without further explanation.	You take on the assignment and have to work overtime. You feel misused and manipulated.

Your partner cannot find the car keys and blames you. You have not touched the keys.

You don't let yourself become upset by this unfair treatment. You try to help find the keys if you think it will keep the peace. You introduce a system for storing the family's keys.	You start a prolonged argument with your partner and bring up the most embarrassing examples from the extensive list of sins and weaknesses.

You are working on more tasks at the same time than you can manage.

You allot priorities to the tasks and start with the most important. You delegate some tasks and if necessary postpone others. You decide that in the future, you will set more realistic goals.	You try to do everything at once. You lose overview, and become tense and irritated. You lower your quality standards and your work is inferior.

You attend a personal development course which contains elements you recognise as being potentially valuable for your future.

You arrive mentally prepared and give your full attention to the course. You are on time in the morning and after each break. You have anticipated possible interruptions, either from home or your company; and you stay until the programme is finished.	You are in contact with your company during each break, and are late after the breaks. You can't concentrate on the programme because you are occupied with other problems. You leave the course an hour before it ends to avoid rush hour traffic. You arrive home $1^1/_2$ hours early, but miss the concluding messages, which could have improved the rest of your life.

OK reaction	Not-OK reaction

You arrive 10 minutes late for an all-day conference with many delegates. The door is closed and you cannot enter the room without being noticed.

Trying not to disturb anyone, you hurry into the room and try to catch up on what you missed.	You wait until the next break before you go in. You sneak in so that no one discovers you arrived late. If anyone sees you, you explain that it wasn't your fault. It was your car, the traffic, the weather, poor directions and your defective alarm clock which prevented you from arriving on time.

You attend a meeting, but feel you are wasting your time. Your presence is not required for the entire session, and you see only a small chance of contributing constructively.

You attempt to move forward the discussion of the topic which demands your presence. You leave the meeting when your topic has been discussed. In the future, you try to avoid similar situations which are a waste of time.	You don't want to offend anyone, so you remain sitting passively throughout the entire meeting. You feel frustrated, and after the meeting, tell your "tale of woe" to colleagues.

You are interviewed by a consultant who has been called in by your company / organisation to advise management on development in the future. In order to give the best possible advice, the consultant must have in-depth knowledge of the present state of affairs.

You answer the questions to the best of your knowledge, providing information which will enable the consultant to function in a professional manner. You stick to your statements and are willing to repeat them at any time, not withholding information for fear of reprisals.	You use the opportunity to air your negative feelings and experiences. You complain and do not mind letting embarrassing episodes and circumstances "slip out". You constantly say to the consultant, "Please don't quote me on this."

You are at a convention, listening to someone present a topic. You don't understand what is being said.

You indicate that you do not quite understand the message and ask for a more detailed explanation.	You don't say anything because you don't want to look stupid. You assume that everyone else understands the message so you try to look as though you too understand.

You probably recognise some of the above situations. You can probably also identify both OK reactions and not-OK reactions in the people around you.

What are your own reactions?
How is your self-esteem?
Where should you concentrate your efforts in order to develop your self-esteem?

Winner or loser?

Someone who feels good about him or herself and functions well with others is called a pearl-fisher in TMI terminology. Psychologists call this kind of person a "winner". A winner sends out OK signals, while a "loser" gives off signals which are not-OK.

In the world of psychology, the words – winner and loser – have a different meaning than in the world of sport, where a winner is selected at the expense of a loser. In the world of feelings, there are either two winners or two losers.

We are all born winners, but as we grow up, we all experience difficulties and disappointments. We record these unpleasant experiences in our brains as "loser tapes" which then limit our opportunities, inhibit our sense of initiative, fetter our resources and create dissatisfaction and frustration.

We ourselves often prevent our own progress. Many people have a tape in their head which keeps repeating:
I can't do it
It can't be changed
I will certainly fail
They think I'm a nobody
It's too late
It's too soon
I'm too young
I'm too old
I can't afford it
There's no use trying
Nobody wants to hear my opinion
It's not easy when you're the oldest child
It's so hard being the youngest
Being the middle child is impossible

I am who I choose to be...

How to identify winner/loser tapes

We have all experienced being winners and losers.
It's important to try to be a winner in as many situations as possible.

Examples of winner tapes and loser tapes

☺ A winner says:	☹ A loser says:
Let's take a look at it.	Nobody knows anything about that.
I'm sure I will find time to do it.	How do you expect me to find the time to do it?
Let's get to the heart of the matter.	Well, it's difficult to give you an exact answer.
I guess I didn't express myself clearly.	You don't understand me.
I made a mistake, but I'll fix it.	It's not my fault.
It looks as though we have different opinions on this matter.	I won't change my mind.
I am OK, but I can be even better.	I'm not as bad as lots of other people.
Let me explain it another way.	As I've said so many times.
There must be a better way.	We've always done it like this in our business.
You're never too old to learn something new.	Do you have any idea how many years' experience I have in this business?
Let's do it right this time.	We've tried this before.
That sounds exciting.	We've never tried that before.

Examples of winner behaviour and loser behaviour

🙂 A winner:	🙁 A loser:
Changes his or her own behaviour.	Tries to change the behaviour of others.
Works hard – and has time to spare.	Is always too busy to do what's necessary.
Knows when to stand firm – and when to give in.	Gives in when it's unnecessary and stands firm when it's not worth it.
Respects other people's abilities and tries to learn from them.	Doesn't recognise other people's abilities, and instead tries to find their weaknesses.
Spends time improving.	Spends time avoiding criticism.
Focuses on opportunities.	Focuses on problems.
Accepts the differences between people.	Doesn't accept the right of other people to be different.
Commits him or herself.	Makes promises.
Explains.	Makes excuses.
Focuses on solutions.	Focuses on apologies.
Speaks up – without interrupting.	Complains about not being able to get a word in.

The greatest pay-off we as losers can obtain from our remarks and behaviour is absolute zero.

Every time you find yourself playing a loser tape, stop and think about how you can change it to a winner tape.

Whenever you find yourself playing a winner tape, you reinforce your OK feeling, pave the way for communication with others, and give them a chance to be winners, too. Everyone wins when you win over yourself.

EXERCISE 8: How to become a winner

Try to list below situations where you have been a loser or a winner. Use examples from both your home and your place of work.

Now make a list of the loser tapes you never want to play again. Write down which winner tapes you will play instead.

When I was a loser:	When I was a winner:

Loser tapes I often use. These are tapes I want to try to stop listening to:	Winner tapes I intend to play frequently instead:

How to develop self-esteem

In order to create a life tree with a strong network of roots, you must develop the most important root of all, your self-esteem.

You are now more aware of your position on the OK attitude scale, of what self-esteem is, and how you can contribute to other people's self-esteem.

When you do this, you strengthen your own OK feeling, and your life becomes richer because you have the capacity to be involved in other people's lives.

In addition, others will be more inclined to appreciate you when you encourage them.

It is not, however, only other people who can encourage you, and thus influence your self-esteem. You too can make an effort to develop your own.

In order to promote this development, you must establish a positive attitude towards yourself and learn to master several techniques. You must seek to enter into a beneficial cycle of thoughts, feelings and actions which strengthen your self-esteem and which reinforce and influence each other in positive ways.

You must learn to like yourself and to see what is unique about you. You must also learn to live in the present without guilt or anxiety. You must be able to see your strengths and make the most of them. Understand that you alone make your decisions and are thus responsible for the situation you are in. You must be flexible and open to new ideas, and learn to vary and change your behaviour. You should look upon problems as exciting challenges and see mistakes and failures as a natural part of the development process. You must think positively and be committed.

Some of the techniques and ideas in the following chapters about the "soil" and "branches" can help you strengthen your own self-esteem and that of others, and thus create a network of roots which give you the best possible conditions for growth.

5. Surroundings

- the soil

This chapter is about how to create fertile soil for your life tree. It deals with how your surroundings – the milieu you live and work in – influence your development, and how you can create a fruitful environment for others in your life.

Surroundings which encourage people to develop are characterised by recognition, tolerance, mutual respect and genuine warmth. An environment which promotes development includes clear goals and guidelines for those who must function together – fostering people's OK feeling, and thus creating winners.

One of the most important questions in psychology is: What factors determine whether a person becomes a winner or a loser?

What makes a winner or a loser?

A person's self-esteem or OK feeling mainly determines whether he/she becomes a winner or a loser.

Your self-esteem is determined by the amount of recognition your brain registers.

Recognition – in its broadest sense – is also called *strokes*.

Strokes are vitally important to the quality of the psychological environment.

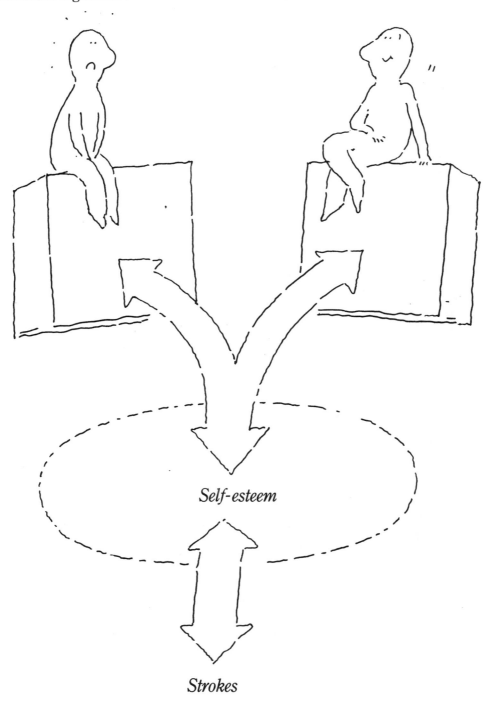

Self-esteem

Strokes

This chapter deals with strokes
– the nourishment the soil around your life tree receives.

What are strokes?

Strokes can be defined as: "Any type of attention people give to one another."

Strokes are the most powerful means we human beings have at our disposal to develop or destroy our own self-esteem or that of others.

It is essential to your well-being that you receive enough strokes because if you do not, you will behave inappropriately, become a loser, or in the worst case, become seriously ill – both mentally and physically.

The way in which you exchange strokes with others determines what kind of relationships you have.

Strokes can be positive or negative, and the relative amount of each determines your *stroke balance* (more about this later in this chapter) which, again, is essential to your self-esteem.

Strokes can be classified by type:
- *Physical strokes:* Paying attention by touching
- *Mental strokes:* Paying attention without touching

Strokes can also be classified by the circumstances in which they are given:
- *Ritual strokes:* Attention determined by a specific event or type of behaviour
- *Spontaneous strokes:* Spontaneous attention

Physical strokes

Physical strokes occur every time the skin is touched, and are very important to the development of the brain, especially in the first years of life.

This is because physical contact or "stroking" stimulates the nerve cells in the skin which transmit electrical impulses to the brain. Stimulating brain cells is vitally important for the development of both the brain and the immune system.

Three examples which demonstrate the importance of physical contact.

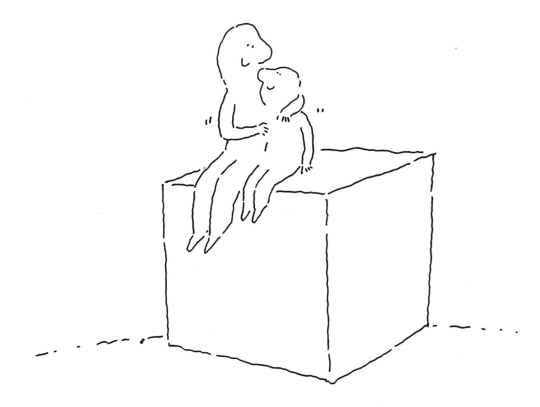

Example 1:
Experiments with monkeys

During the late 70s in the United States, some controversial but epoch-making experiments were carried out with monkeys. Shortly after birth, young monkeys were removed from their mothers. Some were totally isolated from the mothers so that they could neither see, hear nor touch them. Others were placed so they could see and hear their mothers, but not touch them. And finally, some were isolated for longer periods of time, but were allowed to hold their mother's hand through a hole in a glass wall.

During the experiments, all the baby monkeys got plenty to eat from feeding bottles which were put into their cages on poles. All the cages had hard wooden floors, and nothing soft to touch.

The results were both shocking and extremely convincing.

The first group of monkeys became physically and mentally ill during the separation. When they were again allowed to rejoin their mothers, the mental illness diminished slowly, but the physical damage was permanent.

The second group developed behavioural problems. When they were later placed with other monkeys, they displayed anti-social patterns of behaviour, which continued throughout their lifetimes.

The third group also showed obvious signs of injury. When the experiment was over, the brains of the monkeys were examined - all were extremely under-developed or displayed damage.

Example 2:
Babies in incubators

The conclusions from the monkey experiments have been used to explain the great need of human babies for physical contact or "strokes".

For many years, it has been normal procedure to put premature babies into incubators. Such babies usually develop more slowly than full-term babies, and one important reason is the different amount of physical contact these babies receive. A baby in the womb is stroked all over, while one in an incubator only has physical contact on the side it is lying on. Experiments show that if the baby is placed on a sterile sheepskin instead of a sheet and given regular massage, this intense physical contact will stimulate the baby's appetite and quicken its development.

Today, babies who only weigh 6-700 grams at birth survive and develop at a normal rate thanks to the "kangaroo method". The baby is tied to its mother's breast and is in this way touched or stroked intensely. At the same time, the baby can hear its mother's heartbeat.

Example 3: Survival of elderly patients

An experiment conducted at Oxford University Hospital among elderly heart attack patients clearly demonstrated that their chances of survival were greater if they had a dog or a cat when they returned home.

Again, the explanation is the amount of physical contact or strokes the person receives, plus the psychological effect of an animal's acknowledgment of and devotion to a lonely person.

Older people do not touch each other so much, but their skin is stimulated when they stroke their pets.

Touching the skin has a decisive influence on the development of both the brain and body in small children – and has been shown to be vitally important for human beings throughout their lives.

At the beginning of a relationship, people usually touch each other often. Later on, touching and stroking becomes less intense and less frequent. This can lead to major conflicts in the relationship or cause it to break down completely, because, as well as stimulating the brain cells, physical contact is a way of caring and paying attention.

EXERCISE 9: Strokes

Everyone needs physical contact. Think about how you can use your knowledge of strokes both at home and at work for the benefit of yourself and others. Do you give your children enough physical strokes? What about your partner? Do you show enough warmth and affection, or are there too many habits and rituals in your relationship? What about your parents? A little hug now and then, or a pat on the cheek, can work wonders on the people you care for.

Can you give strokes in a natural way at your place of work? A friendly squeeze on the arm or a light touch can have a tremendously positive effect on yourself and others, and light physical contact can have a calming effect on people who are upset. Obviously, strokes must be given naturally, with feeling, and in a manner which is appropriate to the situation, so that motives are not misconstrued. The other person must not get the feeling that strokes are some kind of sexual harassment.

In cultures and countries where people are not so accustomed to physical contact, one must be particularly careful to avoid misunderstandings in connection with strokes. This, however, in no way diminishes the immense human need for physical contact. Lack of touching is certainly one of the reasons why people behave in a chilly manner, and are inhibited or withdrawn.

When you touch someone else, you too receive physical strokes. Furthermore, you can increase your own well-being through massage, bathing, etc.

Give some examples of situations where you can work positively with physical strokes:

Mental strokes

Mental strokes can be defined as any type of attention you can give to or receive from others without touching them. Mental strokes – like physical strokes – are vitally important for a person's development, well-being and behaviour.

Mental strokes can be divided into 3 categories:

- *Positive strokes*
- *Negative strokes*
- *Zero strokes*

Naturally, positive strokes are best for everyone. However, the worst thing that can happen to anyone is not negative strokes, but no strokes at all.

Life has been described as a battle for strokes, whose giving and receiving provides us with something to live for, and makes life meaningful.

When a dog gets positive strokes in the form of hugs, pats, warmth and small rewards, it becomes a calm, harmonious animal and feels good. If it receives negative strokes, it will become fawning or vicious. People are no different in this respect. Fortunately, a dog is so uninhibited that it asks for strokes when it needs them. Every dog owner knows what it's like to be welcomed by a happy, tail-wagging creature every time he or she comes home.

Children have plenty of evidence of their inadequacy: they are too small, can't button their trousers, spill things, and wet the bed. That's why they have such a great need to offset negative strokes. Fortunately, however, children, like dogs, are usually uninhibited enough to ask spontaneously for strokes: "Don't you think I'm wonderful/big/strong/clever?" If children don't receive enough strokes, they will develop devious methods for getting them. For example, a child knows that when you give strokes, you also get them. "Mummy, I love you" is usually followed by "I love you too dear." If children still don't get enough positive strokes, they will work *systematically* to get negative strokes: in spite of everything, these are better than no strokes at all.

Children who are never praised for their school work and whose parents have little time for them develop behavioural problems.

It is a shame that adults have "forgotten" these rules. When they get too few positive strokes, they begin to exhibit various forms of loser behaviour. Smiles disappear, and they start talking about hard times, poor leadership, foolhardy government and bad weather. It would be more appropriate to try to accomplish something and then reap recognition for it.

Positive strokes

Positive strokes raise your self-esteem and make you happy; so any type of positive recognition, attention, praise, appreciation, pleasure, pride or admiration is the best way to create OK-feelings in others. This sounds easy, but it demands a good deal of human insight and experience to give strokes properly.

The effect of positive strokes depends first and foremost on:

- how they are given
- what kind of strokes they are
- when they are given

It can be difficult to give and receive positive strokes in a natural manner, and may demand a lot of practice and thoughtfulness.

The way you give strokes must be adapted to other people, to your own personality, and to the particular situation. Strokes should be given spontaneously, honestly and naturally, avoiding stock phrases and clichés. Be yourself when you give strokes, otherwise the strokes will appear phony to people who know you.

Only *genuine strokes* will be perceived positively. Your heart has to be in it; and you must really feel that the person deserves praise or recognition, otherwise your body language will expose you, and the strokes will be perceived as flattery or as an attempt at manipulation.

Positive strokes don't necessarily have to be awards of honour or include the use of superlatives.

In fact, it's quite simple.

The best stroke you can give is your undivided attention.

Positive strokes have the same effect on human development as sun, rain and fertiliser have on the growth of plants and trees.

You can pay attention in many ways:

- Show by *eye contact* that you:
    - are listening
    - are committed
    - are paying attention completely

- Show by *listening* actively that you:
    - are trying to understand what is being said
    - are trying to understand the other person's thoughts, feelings and motives
    - accept the other person's way of expressing him or herself
    - understand that the other person's intentions are positive
    - are trying to learn something from the other person

- Show *interest* and *commitment* by:
    - remembering other people's names, birthdays, titles, etc.
    - knowing other people's job responsibilities, interests, family members, honorary positions, special needs/wishes, etc.
    - keeping appointments
    - making time for other people
    - knowing your children's school schedules
    - respecting other people's wishes and needs
    - helping and encouraging others
    - avoiding banal activities and empty pastimes

Your attitude towards the person you are giving a stroke to determines how he or she perceives it. Do you really believe the person deserves it – or do you have a hidden motive? Are you trying to flatter or gain something in return for the stroke?

You can become skillful at giving strokes when your attitude is: "I am OK – and other people are OK too, even if they differ from me in various ways. I think that other people deserve strokes when they've made a serious effort – whether or not I get recognition for the efforts I make."

The more strokes you give somebody – the more strokes they feel like giving you.

Give more strokes in those areas important to the other person, which may well be different from those areas important to you. Make an effort to find out what they value. Notice the way they dress, their manner of speaking, their body language, nationality, and social and cultural background, as well as what other people say about them.

Father and son

A father is sitting, reading the newspaper and drinking coffee. His 8-year-old son interrupts him with these words: "Come to my room, Daddy; there's something I want to show you."

The conversation could continue like this:

Dad: "Not right now, I'm reading the newspaper."
Son: "Oh Daddy, won't you please come!"
Dad: "I want to drink my coffee while it's hot."
Son: "Oh come on!"
Dad: "Will you please stop pestering me. Go and get whatever you want to show me and bring it here."

That's not paying attention!

The conversation could also continue like this:

Dad: "That sounds exciting. Here I come!"
Son: "Whoopee!"

Now that's paying attention!

When the father arrives at his son's room and asks, "What did you want to show me?", his son might look around desperately trying to find something.

In a situation like this, some fathers might say, "Why did I have to come all the way to your room when you didn't have anything to show me anyway?"

The father who understands the importance of paying attention understands his child's hidden message. "Daddy, I really want to have to you all to myself. I don't want to have to compete with anybody else. Let's spend some time together. Come into my world."

It's not completely coincidental that a father, and not a mother, was used in the example above. Usually, it's easier for mothers to enter into their child's world than it is for fathers. Surveys also show that most mothers know their children's school timetables while fathers often don't.

Do you know your child's world?

Managers and employees

A manager has attended a course and learned something about the importance of paying attention. He or she then decides to spend more time talking to employees and being visible in the department. The first "victim" of this motivation tour is a computer programmer.

The conversation could be as follows:

Manager: "Good morning, how's everything?"
Employee: "Everything's fine, just fine, thanks."
Manager: "Do you have enough to keep yourselves busy"
Employee: "Yes, in fact we're quite busy at the moment."
Manager: "Well, that's good. Then there's nothing to complain about. It certainly is better to have something to do than to sit around twiddling your thumbs."
Employee: "We're definitely not complaining."
Manager: "It's quite cold today, isn't it? A lot colder than it was this time last year."
Employee: "Yes, you can always hope for better weather, but it's well beyond our control."
Manager: "I know, still I wish we could do something about it. Oh well, I'd better get moving and see how things are in the other departments."
Employee: "Yes, I'm sure you have plenty to look after."

The manager then continues his motivation tour.

That's not paying attention!

The conversation could also be like this:

Manager: "Good morning Jones, it's nice to see you."
Employee: "It's nice seeing you, too."
Manager: "I was just over in the Sales department and they're extremely satisfied with the new programme you developed for them. There's not a single bug in it. Very well thought out. Thank you very much."
Employee: "I'm glad to hear it and glad you appreciate my work."

Now that's paying attention!

If a manager doesn't know what's going on in the different departments, there's no reason to go around advertising it. Employees already know all about their manager's ignorance.

In order to create an environment which promotes development, it's necessary for managers to be interested in their employees' performance and appreciate good work.

Do you pay enough attention to your employees?
Does your manager pay enough attention to you?

Learning to receive positive strokes

Many people miss quite a few positive strokes
because they're not good at accepting them.
    They become self-effacing with comments such as:

- Oh, it was really nothing.
- Don't mention it.
- I did next to nothing.
- I couldn't have done it alone.
- That's what I get paid for.

Are you good at accepting positive strokes?

Don't belittle or underestimate your own efforts.
    Learn to accept strokes good-naturedly.
    Learn to say thank you.
    Learn to say:

- Thanks, I'm glad you appreciate my efforts.
- It was good to be able to contribute to the
  results.
- It's nice working at a place where people
  appreciate your efforts.
- I'm quite pleased with the results myself. I
  really think I have something to be proud of.

If you become better at accepting positive strokes, you
will receive them more often, because those who give
the strokes will feel that you appreciate their recognition.

EXERCISE 10: Giving and receiving strokes

Even though many people find it difficult to give positive strokes, it is probably more difficult for most of us to receive them.

Purpose

This exercise is designed to:

- create a developmental environment for any group of people who must function together on a daily basis – a family, a department, a board of directors, a group of managers, a project-team, a committee, etc.
- improve company culture by helping people with different functions and/or people from different departments to co-operate more effectively.
- improve cooperation in any group of people – build an "attention" culture where each member of the group contributes to strengthening their own and other people's self-esteem.

Results

Participants will understand the importance of strokes for the group's well-being and effectiveness. Participants will learn what the different members of the group want to receive strokes for. Participants will learn to recognise some of the inhibitions which make receiving and accepting strokes difficult.

How to do the exercise

Choose a room which is large enough for the members of the group to move around freely, or do the exercise outdoors.

1. The group members form 2 circles, an inner and an outer circle with an equal number of people in each.
Everyone in the outer circle faces the inner circle. Everyone in the inner circle faces the outer circle. The inner circle is Group A, and the outer circle is Group B.
2. Everyone pairs off, so that each person from Group A is standing face to face with someone from Group B.
3. Next, every Group A person now gives a sincere, positive stroke to the person they are facing.
4. The person from Group B should accept this stroke without reservation, and acknowledge it by repeating the stroke word for word. Something like this: "Thank you very much! I'm glad you appreciate my efforts. I am quite proud of the results myself . . ."
5. Next, the B person adds yet another positive statement about themselves. In other words, the B person gives themselves a positive stroke by describing some accomplishment or skill they really feel they deserve strokes for.

The strokes given during the exercise can pertain to qualities, accomplishments, skills, appearances, attitudes, patterns of behaviour and actions.

6. Repeat the procedure. This time it is Group B's turn to give strokes to the people in Group A. And it's the A people's turn to receive and acknowledge them by saying thank you and then giving themselves another positive stroke.
7. When every pair has completed their exchange of strokes, everyone in Group A takes one step to the left so that they are now facing a new person from Group B.
8. Next, the new pairs exchange strokes – in other words, the whole procedure is repeated. Continue this exercise until everyone from Group A has had a chance to exchange strokes with everyone from Group B. The exercise could also be continued until every person in the entire group has had the chance to exchange strokes with every other person present.

The exercise is not meant to encourage people to go around bragging and showing off, but is designed to encourage members of a group to give and receive strokes, and to recognise their importance to the well-being and effectiveness of a group.

Ritual and spontaneous strokes

Strokes can be classified according to the circumstances in which they are given.

Ritual strokes

Ritual strokes are given because of a specified, predictable event or performance, which is why they seldom come as a surprise and do not have a very strong effect.

Examples of ritual strokes are: Christmas cards, pocket money, birthday presents, sales bonuses, decorations and medals, congratulatory speeches, etc. Obviously these strokes are better than nothing, but they don't necessarily have any strong or long-lasting effect. They are planned and can be taken for granted, sometimes even seeming like empty flattery or as if one person is trying to gain something from another. But even if they don't always bring about outstanding results, extremely negative reactions may arise if they are omitted, and the best results are achieved when their form and content is varied.

Spontaneous strokes

Spontaneous strokes come directly from the heart; and because they are unpredictable, people often see them as stronger, and more genuine and sincere than ritual strokes.

Examples of spontaneous strokes are: an unexpected letter from a good friend, your daughter's happy outburst when you arrive home, a nod of recognition from your boss, an off-the-cuff thank you for good work.

In order to become better at giving spontaneous strokes, you have to work on your attitude towards other people. Get into the habit of reacting immediately when they perform admirably, display positive attitudes, show a sense of commitment, or exhibit good behaviour.

Have you ever had the experience of thinking something positive about other persons when they were not present and feeling that you would like to tell them? But when you saw them the next time, you didn't say anything because you felt the situation just wasn't right to tell them naturally?

It is quite an accomplishment to get into the habit of expressing the positive thoughts you have about others straight away. Praise people at once. If the person isn't there, write them or call them.

Stroke balance

Before discussing the concepts of negative and zero strokes, it is appropriate to consider the concept of a stroke balance.

Every time you receive positive or negative strokes, you register them in your mind in a kind of bank account with a debit and credit side.

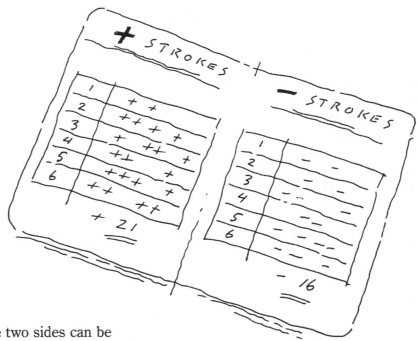

The difference between the two sides can be called your stroke balance. If you have a surplus of positive strokes, you will thrive, be more resistant to adversity, and generally function better. In other words, you will be a winner.

If there is an excess of negative strokes, you will not feel good about yourself, and get along poorly with others. Your stress threshold will be lower and you will be less resistant to adversity. In other words, you will be a loser.

Many types of unusual behaviour and psychological problems can be traced back to a deficit in the stroke balance.

If you don't receive enough positive strokes at work, you will seek them at home. If the number of strokes you receive at work and at home is insufficient, you will seek them when you are at a party, on a business trip, at your club, or in other similar situations. Most of the people who deceive their partners sexually do so not just because they have great sexual appetites, but because the other person gives them too few positive strokes.

If you can't get strokes in any other way, you can buy them. Strokes which are bought are called *status symbols*. Typically, status symbols are only enjoyed when other people can see that you are in possession of them. Examples of things which are often used as status symbols are: cars, houses, saunas, desks, furs, jewelry, uniforms, club memberships, etc.

EXERCISE 11: My stroke balance

Purpose:

To give you an idea of whether you get the strokes you need.

Result:

You will be able to identify what you feel you deserve strokes for. You will become aware of where your needs are met and where they are not being met. You will gain a better understanding of when and why you feel happy or unhappy.

How to do the exercise:

1. On the next page, write down everything you feel you deserve strokes for – both at home and at work. The list should include everything good that you do – as well as all your positive qualities and abilities. Make an effort to think of good things about yourself – even the small things. Include everything which you feel deep down inside that you deserve strokes for, even if ordinarily you are not particularly aware of these things.

2. Examine your list carefully. Put a plus, minus or zero in the space besides each example using the following guidelines:

   $+$ When you feel that:
   - your efforts are rewarded with lots of attention
   - your qualities and skills are appreciated by others and they show their acknowledgement.

   $-$ When you feel that:
   - you receive too little attention for your efforts
   - you are criticised for your behaviour and interest, even if you feel that you are doing your best.

   O When you feel that:
   - you don't receive any attention at all
   - other people have no idea of what you are doing, and they're not interested in knowing either
   - no one is interested in your world in this area.

   Evaluate your situation by balancing the pluses, minuses or zeros.

3. Look at the overall picture. What is the relationship between the pluses, minuses and zeros?
   If you have a surplus of pluses, it indicates that you have a positive stroke balance. If you have too many minuses and zeros, you should work at getting more positive strokes.

4. Do this exercise with the people you live and work with: your husband/wife, members of your family, your boss, your colleagues, your employees. Let them draw up their own lists of things they feel they deserve strokes for.

Exchanging lists and then discussing them can significantly contribute to mutual understanding:

- Why are we the way we are?
- Why do we do what we do?
- How can we avoid hurting each other?
- How can we make each other happy?
- How can we strengthen each other's self-esteem?

At home	Assessment +/−/0	At work	Assessment +/−/0
1		1	
2		2	
3		3	
4		4	
5		5	
6		6	
7		7	
8		8	
9		9	
10		10	
11		11	
12		12	
13		13	
14		14	
15		15	
16		16	
17		17	
18		18	
19		19	
20		20	

I am surrounded by idiots!

A real-life story

One Saturday, the whole family was sitting around the table enjoying lunch together. Suddenly my wife turned pale, and said in an anxious voice, "Oh no, something terrible has happened. You are going to be very angry, and the rest of the weekend will be ruined."

But, I was in great spirits. The food was delicious, the sun was shining, and the birds singing, so I asked, "Why should I be angry?" "I know you," she replied.

"What's happened?" "Just before you came home last night, a client called. I promised you would call back, no matter how late it was. I am so sorry – I forgot to tell you." "No problem. I don't think it's fair that clients should call me in the middle of the night, anyway. I'll call him on Monday. Let's enjoy ourselves. I wouldn't mind another beer." "I'm glad you took it like that. Then you're not at all angry with me?" "No, of course not. Oh, by the way ... who was it?" "It was a director from IBM's international headquarters. He was interested in hearing what you could offer in terms of management training for several different countries." "Why didn't you tell me this to begin with?" "See, now you're angry anyway. I knew it." "What me, angry? Are you kidding? How can I be angry with a woman who has absolutely no brain, a woman who consciously sabotages her husband's work from morning to evening! And who shoves the boulder down again, just when you have finally pushed it all the way up to the top of the mountain." "I didn't do it to upset you." "Of course not. You probably did it because you wanted to help me. You're just like your mother. The whole family is. What kind of a family did I marry into anyway?" "Why do you always get so excited?" "Maybe there's nothing to get excited about, right? You don't understand anything. But I should have learned by now. This isn't the first time. Do you remember last year when you promised to take the keys to the summer cottage? But of course you forgot them so we had to break a window and I cut my hand ..."

"Now you're being completely impossible. I don't want to hear another word about that key!" "You may be right, but a good crime cannot be punished too often!"

On Monday morning I called the client.

He said, "Thanks for calling. I'm sorry I wasn't home Friday evening when I asked you to return my call. We were invited over to our neighbours. I called you to ask you about ..."

I am afraid I forgot to tell my wife about this conversation.

Negative strokes

Negative strokes can take the form of criticism, scorn, ridicule, lack of confidence or ingratitude. They make you feel unhappy, disappointed and inadequate.

Once in a while, it will be necessary to reprimand a member of your family, an employee, a colleague, or a business contact – in other words, to give them a negative stroke.

No one likes to get negative strokes, even if they ask for them. When people ask for criticism, the hidden message is often a desire for attention.

Constructive criticism, however, is not the worst thing a person can get: It is an expression of interest and attention and in many cases helps the person receiving it.

The effect of negative strokes depends primarily on how they are given, when they are given, who gives them, who receives them, why they are given, and what they are given for.

The following recommendations are meant as guidelines, and as a source of inspiration to help you use negative strokes in a positive manner. The suggestions are not described in any logical sequence to be followed step by step for every type of reprimand. Nor is it realistic to consider all the suggestions in every situation.

Don't forget!

When you reprimand others, do so in a manner which allows the other person to change their behaviour without losing their self-esteem.

Both the reprimander and the reprimandee should be in balance emotionally when the criticism is given. The purpose of giving negative strokes should be positive, and not an expression of frustration on the part of the person giving the reprimand.

There must be a positive stroke balance between the giver and the receiver. You can accept and appreciate criticism more easily from a person who usually sees and appreciates your strengths. You probably won't listen to criticism from a person who only notices your weaknesses.

The giver and the receiver should agree that the behaviour in question was inappropriate and should be changed. You should not criticise another person for having opinions which differ from your own or for having done something which that person truly believes was correct. In situations like this, a discussion would be more appropriate than negative strokes.

9 helpful suggestions concerning negative strokes

1. Criticise the behaviour - not the person

Your criticism should concern only the person's behaviour – not the person in question. Show that you feel that the other person is OK, but that their behaviour in the particular situation was not acceptable.

2. Reprimand winners only

Try to avoid giving negative strokes to someone who has a deficit in their stroke balance. First and foremost, this person needs positive strokes. Your criticism could be the last straw. It is more likely that it will cause a negative reaction rather than the desired change of behaviour.

This suggestion is difficult to follow in real life because a loser invites more criticism than a winner does. In addition, it may seem unfair that a loser can get away with things for which a winner would be criticised. Nevertheless, it is more important to turn a loser into a winner than to give everyone the same criticism for the same mistakes.

3. Criticism is the concern of two people

Never reprimand anyone in the presence of others. If you do, you risk having the other person feel ridiculed and put down – they will probably turn a deaf ear to your criticism.

People who witness the criticism of others will probably feel uncomfortable or gleeful. At the same time, they will lose their respect for you and fear they will be your next victim.

4. Negative strokes should be given immediately

Reprimand as quickly as possible – preferably within 24 hours of the so-called "offence". Don't harbour criticism over a long period of time. You run the risk that the other person will forget the unsuitable behaviour and not understand your criticism. In addition, delayed negative strokes can cause great insecurity. The other person feels unsure as to what other unpleasant surprises you have hidden "up your sleeve".

5. Reprimand only on the basis of your own experience

Never criticise another person on the basis of something you have heard but not experienced yourself. You run the risk of creating a major conflict between the person you criticise and the person who "talked". If you allow the people around you to gossip behind each other's backs – and if you join in with the gossip instead of speaking openly to people – it can cause a deep-seated lack of confidence and insecurity to develop around you.

6. Be specific - don't generalise

Stick to the point, and only talk about the particular behaviour in the specific situation. Don't generalise and say things like:

"Can't you ever do anything right?"

"How often do I have to tell you something before you understand?"

"Don't you have any sense of responsibility?"

"Don't you ever think about anyone besides yourself?"

"Why do you always get everything wrong?"

"That wasn't a very bright thing to do."

The other person will only feel that remarks like this are a put down. Such remarks make constructive conversation impossible and will hardly lead to the desired change of behaviour.

7. Don't repeat "old criticism"

Never bring up old criticism according to the motto: "A good crime cannot be punished too often." This will only make the other person feel they were treated unjustly.

It could also provoke despondency and indifference.

"There's no reason to change my behaviour. It won't help anyway. Everyone thinks I'm a blockhead no matter what I do. I can't do anything to change other people's opinions of me."

8. Explain the consequences of the "offence"

It is important that the other person understands the consequences of the offence.

- Explain the danger, risk or other unfortunate effects which are created or which could arise from the offence without exaggerating or playing them down.
- Explain as objectively as possible what damage, losses and other specific problems arose as a result of the person's actions. Be specific in terms of time, amounts and costs.
- Explain your feelings. Why are you reacting as you do? Why are you disappointed, hurt or unhappy?

9. Agree upon how to avoid repeating the same mistakes

Both the giver and receiver should perceive negative strokes as part of a learning process, and as a means of avoiding the same mistakes in the future.

They should agree upon how to avoid repetition, and should both participate actively in formulating the desired change of behaviour.

The giver should assure the receiver that the matter is now completely closed, and that it will never be brought up again.

Even if you follow these suggestions, there is no guarantee that you will achieve the desired effect. It takes much experience and human insight to give another person negative strokes so they produce the desired effect.

On the other hand, every time you succeed in following some of the suggestions for reprimanding, it will be more likely that your negative strokes will have a positive effect.

Learning to accept negative strokes

Don't feel hurt, guilty, anxious, disappointed, aggressive or vindictive when you are reprimanded.

If you are reprimanded and receive negative strokes for mistakes you know you have made, don't try to justify them. Admit your mistakes.

Regard the reprimand as a challenge to improve yourself and as fair treatment.

Regard the reprimand as a helping hand from someone who wants to help you avoid making the same mistake next time.

Don't react negatively if you are criticised or reprimanded for something you are not responsible for. Learn to disregard this criticism. Some day, other people will discover the injustice, and on that day, you will see clearly the advantage of not taking unfair criticism to heart.

Life is too short to let other people's mistakes annoy you. Be content with your own.

Accept criticism when it is justified. Disregard criticism which is not justified.

Regard mistakes and failures as unavoidable and educational aspects of your development.

Learn from your mistakes.

Zero strokes

The best thing a person can receive is positive strokes.

The worst thing a person can receive is not negative strokes – but zero strokes (no strokes at all). Nothing has a more destructive effect on someone's self-esteem and sense of well-being.

A prisoner who is isolated for some offence, is rapidly affected psychologically. If, on the other hand, punishment is given in the presence of other prisoners, this can lead to feelings of importance and the emotion, "You have to admit that I made quite an impression on them."

Lack of strokes has a dramatic effect on people's thoughts, feelings and behaviour. When people don't get enough positive strokes, they try, consciously or subconsciously, to get negative strokes. This reaction is natural because, in spite of everything, negative strokes are better than no strokes at all.

Conflicts at home are often the direct result of a lack of attention; and at work, such a lack can result in high personnel turnover, high absenteeism, lack of commitment and poor quality.

Work which gives zero strokes

Certain forms of work are taken for granted by other people and only receive attention in the form of negative strokes. When the job is done satisfactorily, the person who has done it escapes criticism and is rewarded with zero strokes.

Many forms of perfectly executed routine work generate zero strokes. Such work includes: cleaning, typing, filing, working as a cashier or on an assembly line, packing, and supervising.

And one can literally speak of certain people as having zero strokes jobs: cleaning personnel, bus drivers, dishwashers, EDP operators, and traffic wardens.

Airline cabin personnel obviously receive more strokes for their work than the ground personnel who transport baggage from the aeroplane to the terminal. In most companies, work performed by the sales personnel receives much more attention than work done by employees in the accounting department.

There is a special risk in very large, highly-institutionalised companies that whole categories of employees are forgotten and individual efforts go unnoticed. This is true for people working in for example banks, insurance companies, the postal system, the tax authorities, the customs department and other official agencies.

Let's take a closer look at some of the types of jobs which often receive zero strokes:

Cleaning personnel

It is commonplace to find a large turnover among cleaning personnel.

Cleaning and maintenance are often perceived as a necessary evil and taken for granted. And those who do the job seldom receive any recognition for their work; nor should they expect special attention for average endeavours. Their work has to be very poorly done before anyone reacts at all.

An organisation can achieve a dramatic improvement in the quality of the cleaning, and of the cleaning personnel's well-being and seniority, by ascribing importance to the job and giving it the attention it deserves.

A considerable number of employees at a large cleaning company were celebrating their anniversaries with the firm – and feeling very important. Some of them worked at the local police station, where they had to undergo security checks and wear ID-cards on their uniforms. They cleaned under difficult conditions, around busy policemen and women and desks piled with papers, and surrounded by witnesses and accused. But they didn't "just" clean and make coffee; they infused new energy into the police force and "kept an eye on the country's safety".

Traffic wardens

Traffic wardens are probably not the people who provoke the most cheers and flag-waving when you see them on the street. It's hard to think of a more thankless job.

The often completely innocent traffic warden must accept being the scapegoat for motorists' aggression, "Can't you find anything else to do? Why don't you see to it that we have more parking spaces?"

One must hope that traffic wardens get strokes from their colleagues and bosses for work well done.

When did you last give a traffic warden positive strokes for reminding you that you were violating the law?

The spouse who works in the home

In many couples, it is not unusual for the husband to have two lives, work and leisure, while the wife has three, work, housework and possibly some leisure time.

Housework includes such time-consuming activities as cooking, washing up, ironing, shopping, and driving the children around and is often taken for granted and rewarded with zero strokes.

Another real-life story:

A working wife who always packed her husband's suitcase once said to him, "Do you realise that you've had over 100 travel days this year?" "Have I really?" the husband answered. "It sure has been tough!" "That wasn't exactly what I was thinking of," replied his wife. "I was actually wondering if there was ever anything missing in your suitcase." "No," he answered, a little surprised, "I would have told you if there had been."

Undoubtedly, it would have created a more encouraging environment in that little home if the husband paid more attention to his wife's time-consuming "housework" – even when everything was as it should be.

It would have been more pleasant for him to come home one evening with a bottle of champagne and two glasses, light a candle and say: "Let's celebrate my "travel" anniversary. I've been away 25 times, and my suitcase was packed perfectly every time. I know how long it takes; and I just want you to know how much I appreciate your effort. Thank you!"

There is a chance, in a situation like this, that his wife would answer in a tearful voice: "I do the best I can!" There's also the chance that after all those years, his wife would find her husband's unexpected approach a little too bizarre; in which case, she might give him a lesson in how to pack a suitcase in return for all his attention.

The manager

Many managers receive zero strokes – at least from their employees.

While it is almost looked upon as a duty for a manager to give strokes to employees, it is not as praiseworthy for employees to give strokes to their bosses. There is always the chance that it will be looked upon as flattery, or as an attempt to feather one's own nest.

Employees could certainly improve relations with management and win sympathy for more of their ideas, if they could give management positive strokes naturally, when they deserve them. This would probably also help management listen more carefully to constructive criticism from employees.

Do you notice what your boss deserves strokes for?

Do you give your boss positive strokes?

The waiter

Every day waiters are in contact with many people from whom they receive attention. However, many of these positive strokes are superficial and ritualistic, and are given for the cook's performance rather than the waiter's. Phrases like: "The food is delicious," or "The sauce is delightful," imply that the guests regard the cook's job as commendable while the waiter's is taken for granted – which is why many waiters act in a superficial and ritualistic manner towards the guests.

Everyone has experienced the attitude: "I am sorry, but this is not my table" – as well as indifference, insolence and other "acts of retaliation" from stroke-hungry waiters.

Undoubtedly, guests would receive better service if they gave the waiter strokes for doing the job they are responsible for. Something like: "The food was delicious, and the service was excellent. Thank you for being so kind and attentive."

Learn to notice and appreciate the "obvious"

How many working people in your neighbourhood receive zero strokes for the jobs they do? What kind of efforts are they making? Do you give them enough attention for their efforts, or do you take them for granted?

Learn to recognise that when people "sabotage" something, they are often sending a signal that you are giving them too few strokes.

You can enrich their lives and make them feel important if you make sure they get strokes.
This applies to:
- your husband/wife
- your children and other family members
- your friends and neighbours
- your boss
- your business contacts
- people who play important roles in society (e.g. people who work in schools, government services and institutions)

Try doing as follows:
- Learn to notice and appreciate the work people do
- Try to understand the amount of effort involved
- Show interest in their jobs
- Try to imagine what would happen if their job didn't get done
- Try to imagine that you had to do their job
- Learn to recognise what a substantial part of their lives their jobs take up
- Learn to understand the importance of their efforts in the overall picture

Create an environment in your home and at work where everyone works actively to avoid zero stroke situations, where all kinds of work are considered worthwhile, and every good effort is appreciated.

Create an environment which encourages development – give more strokes

A mental experiment

Sit down in a chair and relax. Close your eyes. Think about your experiences last week. What happened? Who did you spend time with? What did you talk about? How did you feel about yourself? How did you get along with other people?

Did you help to create a positive environment which encourages yourself and others to develop?

Do this mental experiment for each of the people with whom you currently must live and work: your husband/wife, children, parents, siblings, and friends; your employees, colleagues, and boss.

Think about them one at a time and ask yourself the following questions concerning the strokes you gave them during the past week:

- How many times did I give them positive strokes? In what situations? For what? How did I do it? Were they superficial or deeply-felt? Were they spontaneous or ritualistic?
- How many times did I give them negative strokes? In what situations? For what? How did I do it? Did I follow the suggestions for negative strokes? Did they maintain their self-esteem and perceive the strokes as a help?
- What kind of strokes did I give most often last week – positive or negative? What is my stroke balance in relation to the individual person? Does he or she receive mostly positive or negative strokes from me?
- Did they do something last week which I didn't appreciate at all? Did I invest any time in, and show my interest for this person? Do I take their efforts for granted? Did I make any attempts to open the door to their world?

Then ask yourself the following questions about the strokes you received during the past week:

- How many positive strokes did I receive? From my partner? My children? My employees? My colleagues? My boss? My friends?
- How many negative strokes did I receive? From my husband/wife? My children? My employees? My colleagues? My boss? My friends?
- How many times did I make a serious effort without anybody noticing it?
- How many times did I do something for others which they took for granted? Who is interested in my world?

How do you feel right now? What do you feel? Do you give enough strokes? Do you receive enough strokes?

Are strokes something you need to work with? If you do, you will feel better about yourself – and create more friends.

EXERCISE 12: How to give more strokes

Purpose:

To discover what the people around you deserve strokes for, and to ensure that everyone in your life gets the strokes they deserve.

The result:

You become better at giving strokes, and contribute to creating an environment which provides the best possible conditions for well-being and development.

How to do the exercise:

1. List the people with whom you have most contact: your family, friends and colleagues.
2. For each person, list what you think they deserve strokes for.
3. Say when you last gave them a stroke.
4. Indicate when you plan to give them a stroke again.
5. Do it!

Name	What they deserve strokes for	When I last gave them a stroke	When I next plan to give them a stroke	√

Name	What they deserve strokes for	When I last gave them a stroke	When I next plan to give them a stroke	√

Negative reactions to strokes

It is not unusual for people to react negatively when they first receive positive strokes. Here are some examples:

Example 1

A Danish company gave each of their employees six half-bottles of schnapps as a Christmas present.

The first day back at work after the New Year, the managing director happened to hear one of the department heads hurl this remark across the table during lunch, "Wasn't that a wonderful Christmas present? It's a crying shame the supplier seemed to have run out of whole bottles."

Example 2

A woman who stayed at home looking after the children for many years resumed her career.

One evening she came home from work with a bottle of champagne and proposed to her husband that they open the bottle right then and there, and drink it together. "I've been thinking about you all day long," she said, "and I just wanted to be with you. Sometimes I feel we spend too little time together." To which her husband replied harshly, "What have you been doing behind my back?"

Example 3

To celebrate the 100th birthday of its founder, a Scandinavian company invited all employees, both office workers and production crew to a reception at 3 p.m. The invitation mentioned light refreshments and a small, symbolic gift for every employee.

An hour after the invitations were delivered, the production crew stopped working. The reason they gave was that office workers normally work from 9 a.m. to 5 p.m., while the production crew works from 8 a.m. to 4 p.m. By participating in the reception, the production crew would only get one hour off while the office workers would get two. The production crew also notified management that they did not wish to accept any presents.

After the work stoppage, management concluded, "It just goes to show you – there's no point in doing anything special for your employees. It will just be misunderstood anyway."

When you experience a negative reaction from the people you give positive strokes to, it can be tempting to conclude, "Well what do you know? Positive strokes can easily have a negative effect."

This is a hasty and incorrect conclusion: the negative reaction could be for entirely different reasons. It could represent a hidden wish for more strokes, an expression of general frustration caused by a deficit in the stroke balance – or, possibly, the result of a negative balance between you and the person you are giving the strokes to. The person is simply not used to hearing anything positive from you.

If you do not achieve a positive response with your positive strokes, don't lose faith. Continue giving positive strokes, and sooner or later you will see the results. It can take a while to change a negative stroke balance.

Who is my friend?

My friend is interested in me and shows it

•

My friend notices and appreciates my strengths

•

My friend accepts my weaknesses

•

My friend helps me improve

•

My friend listens to me

•

My friend enjoys my success

•

My friend is involved in my everyday life

•

My friend gives to me and receives from me

•

My friend defends me

•

My friend has time for me

•

My friend strengthens my self-esteem

How many friends do you have?

A positive stroke balance is a prerequisite for friendship between two people.

6. My personal goals

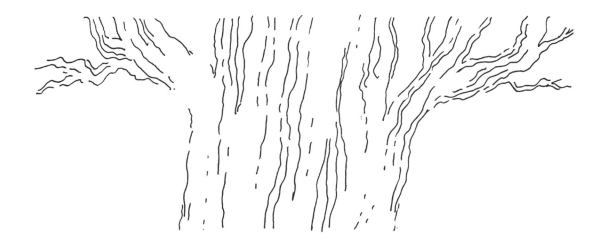

- the trunk

This chapter is about your personal goals – the trunk on your life tree as described in chapter 3.

The importance of having personal goals

A life without goals is a life without meaning. In order for your life to be worthwhile and have meaning, you must have personal goals and continually experience the feeling of working towards them.

Expecting to achieve your goals is a prerequisite for having visions. When you have visions, it is easier to enjoy the present – and to create "pearls".

It is essential to experience success in order to maintain your self-esteem. You experience success every time you achieve a goal or part of a goal.

You must know your goals in order to reach them. If you do not know where you are going, you will never get there.

To decide what one wants out of life is so difficult that many people never work it out. Most people want more out of life, but do not know exactly what this "more" is.

When people have a goal, it is often a material goal: a larger house, a better job, more money, or a nicer car. Seldom do people realise how to make life more meaningful, or how to improve relations with others.

Be sure not to overestimate the importance of material goals. It will undoubtedly give you much more self-esteem and make your life more meaningful if you achieve non-material goals – such as learning new skills, spending more time with the people who are important to you, daring to say what you mean, and doing what you really want to do.

We often let ourselves drift down the stream, guided by chance – or by what we believe to be chance – as situations arise – one by one. We think we are lucky if we get a more lucrative job, are transferred to another department, or find a house we can afford.

But life does not have to depend on chance. To a great extent, you can create your own opportunities if you just give yourself the time to figure out what you want.

Even if reaching goals is important, enjoying the journey towards those goals is more important.

My "tunnel-life"

One man's account of his journey through life

My career

Just before I began school, I looked forward to the first year tremendously. My older sister was in the second year. I stayed home all day with our nanny.

When my big sister came home from school, I got a glimpse of the exciting world outside: school. I couldn't wait until it was my turn. I was in no doubt: happiness was located somewhere in the school. The time before my first day felt like a journey through a dark tunnel, at the end of which I could catch a glimpse of light – the light from the world of school.

Finally the great day arrived when my new, happy life was supposed to begin. My first school day. It almost lived up to my expectations. In fact the whole first week at school almost did.

But gradually, as time went by, and the demands on me and the other innocent victims increased, I realised that I was not yet in the valley of happiness. The light I had seen at the end of the tunnel was apparently bogus light from the sky which had strayed in from a crack in the tunnel.

I continued my journey through the tunnel and it wasn't long before I began to sense where happiness really lay. By listening to people who had left school long ago, I saw more and more clearly that happiness was getting out. Gradually, I could again see the light at the end of the tunnel – the light which signalled the last day of school.

I didn't really want to continue my education after primary and secondary school, but my plans to leave school for the happiness which presumably existed in the pulsating world of business were abruptly frustrated. I fell hopelessly in love with the girl who sat next to me in class, and she was determined to continue her education. It wasn't long before she convinced me that happiness was spending the next 3 years at school with my true love.

Gradually as the demands of teachers grew, my picture of happiness began to crack. Nevertheless, a new light soon began to shine at the end of the tunnel – the last day at school. I was no longer in doubt. Happiness was putting the 6th form behind me and finishing school.

When I graduated, all the doors of life opened for me. My uncle, who was an officer in the military reserve, convinced me that every young man with any respect for himself should dedicate a part of his life to serving his country and people. So began my life as a recruit. Happiness smiled upon me.

My lofty thoughts of togetherness, the fighting spirit, and love of country soon suffered some serious defeats. I woke up to the life of an enlisted man with drill, cleaning, impossible orders, trials of stamina, military food and other humiliations.

My journey through the military service still today represents the darkest stretch of my tunnel journey. Nevertheless, there was light ahead. The countdown progressed with all certainty, day after day, right until my last day as an enlisted man. When I crawled out of the tunnel and out of uniform, my best friend from my army days helped me find happiness. He thought a degree in business administration would bestow un-dreamt of opportunities upon me. There was no doubt in my mind – he was right.

It took me a whole month to realise that I had been tricked into a new tunnel where the only saving thought was the hope of passing the final exams and graduating.

Finally, with my degree in my hands, I stood at the pinnacle of happiness. Now I was going to enjoy life, and I really did. For one whole week, life was a party, that is, until I started to feel restless. An important decision had to be made. I had to find a job I could be happy doing.

I was lucky. I found a job as assistant to the managing director of a line of chain stores. Since I had a degree in marketing, the M.D. found it perfectly natural to terminate his agreement with the chain's window dresser. The prestigious job of decorating the windows of all the chain's 40 shops every six weeks was bestowed upon me. I didn't even have to think for myself because the M.D., who was very interested in design, decided how the windows should look – down to the very last detail.

Once, while I was decorating a Christmas window on the main shopping boulevard, I fell right through the bottom of the window down to the cellar along with the flags and Santa Clauses – to the great amusement of all the people passing by.

While I was lying down in that cellar recovering, I suddenly saw the light at the end of the tunnel. I realised that happiness was finding a new job where I could put my education to better use. I kept looking for happiness in the next 3 jobs I had, but my "tunnel-life" was darkened by the intrigues of my colleagues and by the inability of my bosses to understand my genius.

I am still looking for a job where I can be happy.

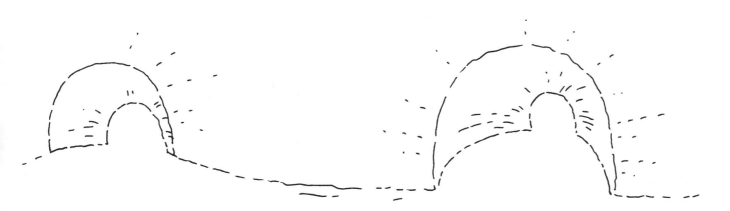

My place of residence

My family and I are also looking for a house where we can live happily.

When my wife and I got married, we thought we had found our ideal home when we moved into a magnificent 2-bedroom apartment with a view over a marsh with wading birds. Happiness resided with us for a whole month. Then the wind changed direction: happiness disappeared with the breeze, and was replaced by the unbearable stench of a polluted swamp.

We escaped through the tunnel and finally found happiness in a brand-new terraced-house with a view to the south. However, the feeling of happiness was somewhat lessened by the noise from our neighbours; and by the lawn which was a chapter unto itself. The excavators had compressed the earth so tightly that life was difficult for the worms. It would take many years before our property could be transformed into a tropical paradise. It was more probable that happiness would turn up in a detached house with a large, old garden.

That journey was completed in less than 7 years.

If our new house had only had an outdoor swimming pool, our search for happiness would have ended.

After 4 years, we dipped our toes for the first time into the ice-cold water of our own swimming pool. It was wonderful – the whole day long, however, our plans to swim the next day were frustrated by having to remove all the leaves and other debris from the pool; and our expectations were disappointed once more. The weather in Denmark is not suitable for outdoor swimming pools.

But we were closer to happiness than ever before. The only thing which stood between us and happiness was owning a house with an indoor swimming pool.

Six years later, the dream came true – almost.

Until Thursday, I thought happiness was living here in our new house, but it turns out that the chemicals in the pool are corroding all the plumbing and metal fittings in the entire house.

My children

When we were first married, my wife and I agreed that happiness was having children. And so it was. But having small children is not always happiness. They limited our freedom so we looked forward to the day when the oldest was big enough to take care of the youngest. Then we'd be able to do the things we did before they were born. That time came soon enough, except that our oldest didn't feel like taking care of the youngest.

So we decided that happiness was having two children who were big enough to take care of themselves. It wasn't long before this wish was also granted.

Now the way was clear for a happy family life where everyone could enjoy spending time together to the fullest. The problem was that the children didn't really feel like spending time with their parents, they had their own careers to pursue. Each of us had our own definition of happiness. To a certain extent, my wife and I could understand our children's desire to spend more time away, than at home. Their rooms were not that big.

Our dream of a bigger house with room enough for everyone became a reality one week before our eldest moved out.

When our youngest child moved away, we both agreed that happiness was being able to afford a good education for the children; and maybe some financial assistance to ensure their happiness.

We were proud that we could afford to help them financially, as not all children receive this kind of help. Nevertheless, a bit more gratitude would have cast a little more light into the tunnel.

Now we are just looking forward to having grandchildren. There is probably no greater happiness than having grandchildren. I hope for my grandchildren that their parents will be able to afford to help them with their education in the same way we helped ours.

...But my wife and I still believe we'll find happiness. If only we can find a smaller house – without a swimming pool – and I get a new job. And if our children do get a good education and pass it on to their own...

The story of this voyage was told by an explorer of life who finally discovered that it is more important to enjoy the journey towards goals than to reach them.

Do you recognise this story?

An incorrect attitude to goals is what leads us into the tunnel, while the right attitude makes life an exciting journey filled with interesting experiences and beautiful sights each and every day.

To My Grown Up Son

My hands were busy through the day,
I didn't have much time to play.
The little games you asked me to,
I didn't have much time for you.

I'd wash your clothes, I'd sew and cook.
But when you'd bring me your picture book
And ask me please to share your fun,
I'd say "a little later son."

I'd tuck you in all safe at night
And hear your prayers, turn out the light,
Then tiptoe, softly to the door,
I wish I'd stayed a minute more.

For life is short and years rush past,
A little boy grows up so fast,
No longer is he at your side,
His precious secrets to confide.

The picture books are put away,
There are no children's games to play,
No good night kiss, no prayers to hear,
That all belongs to yesteryear.

My hands, once busy now lie still,
The days are long and hard to fill,
I wish I might go back and do
The little things you'd asked me to.

Alice Chase

Setting personal goals

In order for life to have meaning, it is important to have goals and to reach them. However it is not just a question of reaching goals, but of enjoying the journey towards them. It can be difficult to define your goals – especially the intangible ones.

The rest of this chapter deals with how you can set overall goals for yourself and reach them.

What is a goal?

A goal is a description of a condition one wishes to achieve, the situation you want to be in when you have carried out certain actions.

"Losing weight" is not a goal because it does not describe a condition or situation you wish to achieve. However "to be able to wear my party dress" or "to weigh 70 kg" by the first of April next year are.

A goal should be described in such a way that you know when it has been achieved; because if you do not know when you have reached a goal, you will not be able to enjoy it.

Many people have no goals. Instead, they are guided by an eternal striving for something bigger, something better, something more, and all the rest. So long as this "bigger, better, more and all the rest" is not translated into goals, it is difficult to be satisfied with one's own life and efforts.

A person whose ambition is to earn more money may be a high-achiever, but he or she has no goals. Someone like this probably will not be happy until they have acquired all the money in the world.

Unfortunately, many people do not need goals in order to continue striving – all they need is to be pointed in the direction of "bigger, better, more and all the rest".

A lack of goals typifies the behaviour of many people whose actions end up being nothing but a kind of empty striving for the sake of activity alone. This can lead to an eternal, self-destructive struggle. Usually something happens in a person's life which puts a stop to this endless, empty striving.

People who realise that the greatest part of their life is over also understand that all their previous striving did not bring them happiness. Some cling desperately to the past and talk about the good old days. Others have learned to concentrate on enjoying the present.

The sooner a person learns to set real goals – both material and non-material – and work towards them, the more meaningful life will become.

Guidelines for goal-setting

You will be more likely to achieve your goals if they fulfill the following conditions:

A goal must be clearly formulated

A goal must describe the situation you desire as clearly and as specifically as possible.

A goal must be realistic

A goal must be grounded on reality. It should be possible to achieve the goal within a reasonable framework.

A goal should be challenging

You must make an extra effort to reach your goal. You have to try harder.

It is important to create a balance between what is realistic and what is challenging. Most people can manage more than they think they can.

When you set your goals, do not be afraid to go a little further than what you believe you can achieve.

A goal should be worthwhile

Achieving a goal must be important to you. It should have a high priority; otherwise you might easily be tempted not to make the effort required to reach it.

Which goals should I set for myself?
Both large and small goals. Short-term and long-term goals. Material and non-material goals.

You should also get into the habit of continually setting goals for different periods: the day, the week, the month, the year, and your whole life.

Your goals will constantly change, depending upon your age and your experiences. This is why you should adjust your long-term goals at least once a year.

You are more likely to achieve your goals if you:

- Write down your goals
- Determine which activities you must do to achieve them
- Set deadlines for these activities
- Be sure to use your time and energy on precisely these activities

Checklist: My personal goals

Your overall goals can be defined within 7 main categories:

1. **Health and well-being**

2. **Education and skills**

3. **Job and career**

4. **Financial circumstances and material possessions**

5. **Relationships**

6. **Attitudes towards life and values**

7. **Use of time**

On the following 7 pages you can define your personal goals for each main category – either alone, or with your husband/wife or with a good friend.

1. Health and well-being

List below your personal goals in relation to health and well-being.

Let yourself be inspired by the following words and phrases:

Physical fitness. Weight. Eating habits/ nutritional needs. Smoking/drinking habits. Relaxation. Medical examinations. Body care. Clothes.

My goals	My sub-goals

2. Education and skills

List below your personal goals in relation to your education and skills.

Let yourself be inspired by the following words and phrases:

Formal education/degrees. Further education. Professional updating. Language skills. Background knowledge on cultural/economic/political/social affairs. Written/oral communication skills. Practical skills. Technical skills. Understanding of human relations.

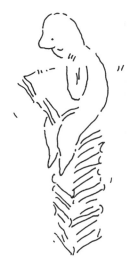

My goals	My sub-goals

3. Job and career

List below your personal goals in relation to your job and career.

Let yourself be inspired by the following words and phrases:

Choice of occupation/line of business. Career. Desire for influence. Responsibility. Challenges. Variety. Security. Environment. Salary. Working hours. Benefits. Retirement. Sabbatical leave. Vacations. Location. Commuting distance. Opportunities for personal development.

My goals	My sub-goals

4. Financial circumstances and material possessions

List below your personal goals in relation to your financial circumstances and your desire for material possessions.

Let yourself be inspired by the following words and phrases:

Income. Security. Money management. Liquidity. Taxes. Investments. Savings. Accumulation of property. Independence. Retirement plan. Life insurance. Private/joint property. Wills. The next generation. House/flat. Car(s). Boat(s). Summer cottage. Furniture. Equipment/furnishings. Decoration/art work. Clothing. Private consumption. Travel.

My goals	My sub-goals

5. Relationships

List below your personal goals for your relationships with others.

Let yourself be inspired by the following words and phrases:

Husband/wife. Children. Grandchildren. Parents. In-laws. Brothers. Sisters. Nieces/nephews. The rest of the family. Division of chores at home. Career/family life. Family patterns. Lifestyle. Friends. Society. My boss. Colleagues. Employees. Business contacts. Authorities. Organisations. Clubs. Politicians. Opinion-makers. The media.

My goals	My sub-goals

6. Attitudes towards life and values

List below your personal goals in relation to your attitudes towards life and values.

Let yourself be inspired by the following words and phrases:

Self-knowledge. Commitment. Tolerance. Self-esteem. Self-confidence. Sense of responsibility. Control of own life. View of human nature. Attitudes towards others. Political convictions. Ethics. Integrity. Religion/faith. Ideology. Group affiliation. Present situation. Respect. Dignity. The opinion of others.

My goals	My sub-goals

7. Use of time

List below your personal goals in relation to how you use your time.

Let yourself be inspired by the following words and phrases:

Relation between working time and leisure time. Between time spent on oneself and on others. Between time spent on maintaining the status quo and developing something new. Relation between performance and enjoyment. Leisure activities. Hobbies. Club work. Sports activities. Political activities. Travel. Holidays. Social activities. Traditional activities. Variety in life. Effective use of time. Quality time.

My goals	My sub-goals

MORE HASTE -

Inscription for a monument
at the crossroads

Here lies, extinguished in his prime,
a victim of modernity:
but yesterday he hadn't time –
and now he has eternity

                    Piet Hein

How to translate aspirations into action

On the preceding 7 pages, you have listed some of your personal goals. These express some of your deepest desires and aspirations.

It is important that you do not let them remain as aspirations only. It would be very unfortunate if your goals suffered the same fate as Mr. and Mrs. Nicholson's New Year's resolutions.

The same old story as last year

Once again, the time had finally arrived. The whole Nicholson family was gathered in the living room around the television. The champagne was ready. It was 4 minutes to midnight. Peace had descended over the party and Mr. Nicholson, who had eaten and drunk a little too much, was sitting holding his belly. Mrs. Nicholson was staring out into space. Her eyes were caught by the light of the candles on the table. There was a faint suggestion of a smile on her lips and a thoughtful expression on her face. She signals to Mr. Nicholson to open the champagne. The glasses are quickly filled with sparkling liquid.

Everyone gets up. It is finally time. The clock strikes 12 and heralds the start of the new year. Everyone drinks to each other's health. Hugs and Happy New Year greetings are exchanged. Mrs. Nicholson goes quietly over to Mr. Nicholson. She has tears in her eyes. She squeezes his hand and whispers emotionally in his ear: "Next year... we must spend more time with the children." Mr. Nicholson returns her warm squeeze. He looks at her understandingly – he is deeply moved and nods his head in approval.

Later that night, after all the guests have gone home, he confides in her, "Next year I will start studying French seriously, and I am going to get into better shape physically." Mrs. Nicholson vows she will do everything she can to support him in carrying out his New Year's resolutions; then she reveals her own plans to him. Next year, she is going to take up her old hobby again, and in addition spend more time with her parents. The atmosphere between Mr. and Mrs. Nicholson is warmer and more intimate than it has been for a long time. Optimism, visions and new challenges are in the air. Mr. and Mrs. Nicholson are going to create a better life and become completely new people. Just before they switch off the light over their bed, they promise each other – apart from eternal fidelity – to do away with all those passive evenings spent in front of the television and start arranging some meaningful family activities instead.

Mr. and Mrs. Nicholson's New Year's resolutions are so good that they use the same ones every year.

How do your New Year's resolutions fare? Are they a sign that next year is going to be the same old story as last year?

The important thing is to transform your aspirations into actions.

The Daruma doll

The Daruma doll from Japan is a "toy" for people who want to achieve their goals.

In place of eyes, there are 2 white spaces in which the doll's owner draws the pupils - one at a time. The first pupil is drawn in when a goal is set; the second when it is accomplished. In between, the missing eye will remind its owner that the goal has not yet been reached, and consequently inspire the person to action.

The Daruma doll was named after an Indian prince who was famous for his self-discipline and positive outlook on life. The doll is widely used today in the Far East, where it is looked upon as an effective results tool.

Many companies in Japan have giant Darumas standing in each department. When a new goal is set, every employee writes his or her name on the Daruma doll, and the one eye is drawn in. When the goal is reached, the other eye is drawn in and all the employees dance around the doll and sing a special Daruma song.

My personal goals for next year

Go through the goals you have listed on the previous pages for each of the 7 main categories.

Choose those which you feel are the most important – the ones you intend to achieve within the next 12 months. Be sure that your goals meet the conditions listed on page 101. List below your goals for next year.

The purpose of making a list of your goals is not to give you a guilty conscience; so don't write down more goals than you believe you can manage. You should have some goals left over for next year!

Put a deadline on each goal. Goals without deadlines have a tendency to be left unfinished.

Remember a goal should describe a situation you wish to achieve and not just a search for "bigger, better, more, and all the rest".

When you are resolved to achieve your goal, you can pencil in one of the Daruma doll's eyes in the scheme below. You will find a description of the Daruma doll on the previous page.

My goals for next year	My deadline

to be continued

My goals for next year	My deadline

7. My knowledge and skills

- the branches

This chapter deals with your knowledge and skills – the branches on your life tree as described in chapter 3.

The more knowledge and skills you have, the richer your life will be.

On the next pages, you will find inspiration and techniques to help you add more branches to your life tree.

This chapter contains the following topics:

● Driving licence to the world of feelings
● Tolerance
● Quality time
● Variety
● Stress control
● Rapport and pacing

This list is in no special order. On the next pages, you will find an introduction to each topic, meant to inspire you to delve more deeply into the topics you find most interesting.

This list represents a small sample of the knowledge and skills you can acquire.

To continue your personal development, you must find more topics yourself, and deepen your knowledge of these by continually reading and learning more about them.

Here are some suggestions for branches you can add to your life tree:

– language skills
– presentation and communication skills
– writing skills
– computer skills
– planning and organisational skills
– delegation skills
– negotiation skills
– self-discipline
– creativity
– sports
– music
– art
– leadership skills
– hobbies
– flexibility
– professional know-how
– the art of cooking
– and so on.

Driving licence to the world of feelings

Everyone is constantly faced with problems large and small which must be solved. These problems can be divided into two categories, depending upon whether they are more concrete in nature or more emotional.

Concrete problems come from the "world of facts" and can usually be dealt with by rational methods, experience and professional or technical know-how.

Problems from the "world of feelings" take longer to deal with. They are more difficult to see through. They hurt, and create frustration. All in all, they cause us more worry than problems from the world of facts.

EXERCISE 13: Problems in the 2 worlds

The purpose of this exercise is to increase awareness of where your most difficult problems arise – in the world of feelings or the world of facts.

On the chart on page 117, list in the left hand column some of the more difficult problems you are experiencing right now, or have experienced during the last 12 months.

In the next column, describe the factors – as you see them – which go into making up this problem, and try to describe the causes as you experience them.

Indicate – by placing an × in one of the two columns to the right – whether you think the problem comes from the world of facts or the world of feelings.

The square symbolises the world of facts. The heart symbolises the world of feelings.

Problems from the world of facts are concrete, tangible problems which are usually easy to describe in a rational and objective manner. These problems are technical, economical or professional.

Problems from the world of feelings are completely different. They are often difficult to describe and make tangible because they depend on the individual's attitudes and experiences. These problems are related to, e.g. co-operation, communication, relationships and feelings.

Problem I am experiencing	The problem's factors and causes	□	♡

The world of feelings

It is probably not so strange that problems in the world of feelings are the most difficult to solve.

Most people in the Western world have some level of education in topics concerning the world of facts: accounting, mathematics, geography, physics, chemistry, biology, history, and languages; as well as economics, technology and law. In addition, there are the commercial subjects such as marketing, purchasing, EDP, logistics and production; and the business-oriented subjects: retailing, the various crafts, the service industry, etc.

Very few of us have any formal education in the "workings of the human mind", in the ways of thoughts and feelings, and in the chemistry and communication which takes place between human beings.

We do not know enough about how to inspire and motivate each other. Or about how to communicate so that others understand, or how to create visions and develop creativity. Or how to deal with conflicts and tense situations, how to achieve enthusiasm, satisfaction at work, pride, tolerance and flexibility. Or how to create feelings of togetherness and a team spirit.

The results of our lack of knowledge are difficulties in co-operating, divorce, poor relationships, illness, increased absenteeism, vandalism, crime, conflicts, stress, increased personnel turnover, lack of confidence, dissatisfaction, lack of commitment, low productivity, mistakes/errors, unnecessary expenditure, poor quality, etc.

In order to feel good about ourselves and to get along well with the people around us, we should all learn something about the rules which apply in the world of feelings. Why am I the person I am? Why do I do what I do? How can I improve the way I feel about myself and the way I get along with others?

Leaders and managers of the future will no longer be able to survive with an education solely to do with the world of facts, because one of a leader/manager's most important tasks is to inspire employees to do their best at work. This demands insight into human nature, credibility, a sense of ethics, communication skills and pedagogic/educational abilities.

In the world of facts, you can manage by reading *"on the line"*.

In the world of feelings, you must also be able to read *"between the lines"*.

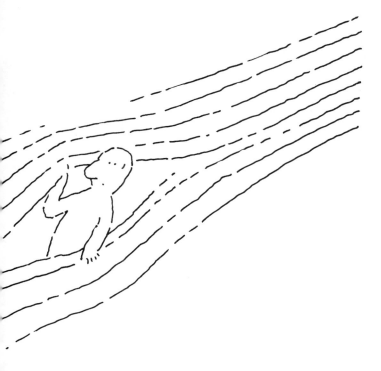

In the world of facts, words and phrases such as the following are used: plans, leaky water pipes, school schedule, budget, invoice, percentage, article 17 section 2, market share, economy, stock of goods, balance of payment, "this is not in agreement with current regulations", "the gross national product has risen by 0.4% in spite of a slump in the market", "if you make a greater effort, the company's competitive power will be strengthened".

In the world of feelings, words and phrases such as the following are used: consideration, attention, sorrow, happiness, bitterness, love, hate, pride, wonderful surroundings, a great view, lovely weather, "It makes you feel great", "I'm so happy to hear it", "I understand you are angry", "I have confidence in you", "I would like to hear your advice", "I know how much work went into the job you've done", "...and to hear something like that from you", "I won't stand for it anymore", "You should be ashamed of yourself", "I'm really sorry it didn't turn out better, I did the best I could", "I saw your daughter yesterday, she's so pretty, she looks just like you".

When you are moving through the "traffic" on your journey through life, it's well worthwhile having a driving licence for both the world of facts and the world of feelings.

We call a person who can move about in only one of the two worlds a "one-track person".

Someone who can move about in both worlds we call a "both/and person".

On the next pages are some examples of the differences in behaviour exhibited by these 2 types of people.

Situation 1: An employee's family

An upset employee goes to his boss and says, "I have to leave work for a few hours because one of my children got hurt and has been rushed to hospital."

The one-track person's reaction
The one-track person says, "I see. *I suppose you have to go to hospital when your children are sick. If it's not serious, I want you back before long. The day has hardly begun.*"

The both/and person's reaction
The both/and person says, "I'm so sorry to hear that. Is it Tom or Karen?

...I hope it's nothing serious. Go right now. Forget about your work. We'll take care of whatever comes up while you are gone – and drive carefully.

And...please call me when you know something more. I would like to know how everything is."

How would you have reacted in the above situation?
How would your boss have reacted?

Situation 2: The birthday

Bridget, a department manager, is sitting eating lunch with her secretary, Elizabeth, and several colleagues, one of whom says, "Did you know it's Elizabeth's birthday today?"

The one-track person's reaction
The one-track person says, slightly surprised, "No, I didn't know." And then turns to her secretary, "Is that really true? Is it your birthday today?"

After confirming that the statement is correct, the one-track person says, "Well that just goes to show you. We're all getting older. In fact, I was at a birthday party at my cousin's place last Thursday. They've just bought a new house on a very favourable mortgage. You know, it's not a bad time to buy at the moment..."

The both/and person's reaction
The both/and person smiles and nods.

Then the secretary replies, "Bridget was waiting by the front door to congratulate me when I arrived at work this morning. I also got a bouquet of flowers from the whole department."

The both/and person adds, "As you probably know, we are all very glad to have Elizabeth with us."

How would you have reacted in the above situation?
How would your boss have reacted?

EXERCISE 14: One-track and both/and reactions

Below you will find several different situations.

For each situation, describe how you think the 2 different types of people would react.

Use extra paper if necessary.

Also think about:
How would you have reacted in the situations below?
How would your boss have reacted?
How would your husband/wife have reacted?

Situation 1

A child comes home from school with a letter from the teacher, from which it is clear that the child's performance is far from satisfactory. The letter mentions that the child is a great soccer player, but, the teacher stresses, has difficulty concentrating in class and seems uninterested and lazy. For example, the teacher says the child is doing very poorly in German and maths.

How do the parents react?

The one-track person's reaction	The both/and person's reaction

Situation 2

A company has had a good year with very satisfactory financial results, but the employees have not yet heard the good news. Since management has decided that the employees should benefit, the managing director has asked the personnel manager to put forward a proposal as to what can be done for the employees and how the news should be communicated to them.

How does the personnel manager react?

The one-track person's reaction	The both/and person's reaction

Situation 3
Employees in one of the company's branch offices have long been discontented with conditions at work. Headquarters finally receives a letter from the branch manager, from which it is clear that the branch receives far too little information from headquarters.
    How does the responsible person at headquarters react?

The one-track person's reaction	The both/and person's reaction

Situation 4
A group of friends are gathered together for a festive occasion. A newcomer begins telling a very old and widely known joke with great enthusiasm and colourful body language.
    How do the people in the group react?

The one-track person's reaction	The both/and person's reaction

Situation 5
A seminar, held for a large group of people, is excellent in many ways. The presentation is dynamic and entertaining, and the content is particularly relevant. Unfortunately there are minor faults, including a number of spelling errors in the seminar material.
    How do the participants react?

The one-track person's reaction	The both/and person's reaction

"Traffic regulations" in the world of feelings

In order to feel good about yourself and to get along well with other people, it is important to learn the traffic regulations which apply to the world of feelings.

These "regulations" are dealt with in depth in the next chapters of this book.

Here are some examples. Regard them as preparation for further travel.

"You are rarely angry for the reasons you think."
Anger is a natural human reaction and can actually be a sign of health.

When people are angry, their feelings have been hurt in one way or another. Anger is an expression of irritation, regret, disappointment or frustration of some kind. It doesn't matter a great deal if one expresses anger spontaneously, as long as it passes quickly and doesn't cause any long-term inappropriate behaviour or bitterness in one of the persons involved.

Things which make our feelings boil over can be difficult to describe or explain to ourselves. The cause of the frustration can be a series of events or experiences which have built up over a period of time, making it difficult to point to one specific cause.

When we express anger and frustration, we are usually aware of the fact that it is somewhat unfortunate; and since anger itself can be experienced as a defeat, many people try to justify it, or rationalise it in ways that are acceptable both to their surroundings and to themselves.

Whatever reasons people claim for their anger they are seldom the complete explanation. Often their explanations only scratch the surface – but some happen to be the straw which breaks the camel's back.

In order to cope with people who are angry, and to help them deal with their irrational, negative and destructive behaviour patterns, it is essential to find the deep-seated reasons for their anger.

In order to discover if someone is really dissatisfied for the reasons they give, one can try to deal with the problem as stated. If this does not bring about a positive change in the angry person's behaviour, it is almost certain that there is something more to the anger than the apparent explanation.

For instance, let us say that employees complain about not receiving enough information from management.

Let us presume that management takes this complaint seriously and tries to correct the problem by supplying more information. If, in fact, a lack of information is only the apparent cause of the employees' frustration, more could easily lead to a reaction such as, "How can we do our jobs properly when we are swamped with information all the time?"

"You are seldom angry for the reasons you think."

**"The opposite of love is not hate
- but indifference."**

If your husband or wife says, "I hate you!" – there's still hope.

If your partner is angry at you, it demonstrates that, in spite of everything, he or she still has certain feelings for you.

It is much worse if you come home three hours late and your partner only says, "No big deal. I hardly noticed you were gone."

Being hurt or disappointed once in a while, or having difficulty controlling our tempers on occasion, probably cannot be avoided. Sometimes we even hurt the people who mean the most to us: our family, friends and colleagues.

Spontaneous anger and "small outbursts" are hardly worth worrying about, as long as they do not develop into long-term, negative patterns of behaviour, spitefulness, suppressed hatred, or paranoia – in fact they may even add a little spice to life.

Once in a while, it is better to let off steam and express your anger than to let bitterness, disappointment and other frustrations remain locked up inside.

Indifference has by far the most detrimental effect on relations between men and women and on close co-operation between people.

There is reason to worry if you say to your husband or wife, "Kiss me," and get the answer, "What time is it?"

An exchange between husband and wife: She asks, "Why don't you ever tell me anymore that you love me?" He answers, "I told you on our wedding night. If I change my mind, I will be sure to let you know!"

Tolerance

Many of the conflicts which arise between people who must live and work together occur because we are all different.

For instance, one person has every aspect of his or her life neatly organised, while the next person is scatterbrained and disorderly.

Another person is very tolerant, while someone else has difficulty accepting any kind of behaviour which might deviate from their own norms.

Conflicts arise because people have difficulty accepting the behaviour and attitudes of others.

EXERCISE 15: Learning to live with people's differences

The following exercise can prevent conflicts and clear the air between 2 people. The exercise is ideal for:

- couples
- parents/child
- employees/boss
- friends
- colleagues
- neighbours
- etc.

Purpose

To learn how to improve relations with another person. In this exercise, "the other person" is called your "partner."

Becoming aware of, and learning to understand more fully, the areas where you and your partner are alike or differ, will improve your relationship.

The word "areas" refers to attitudes, behaviour, values, likes, dislikes, interests, abilities, skills, background, origin and experiences.

Result:

- You are able to enjoy your similarities.
- You map out your differences.
- You create an opportunity to give each other recognition for the differences you value.
- You create an opportunity to correct those differences which one of you finds difficult to accept.
- Unacceptable differences become less striking when they are seen in relation to the differences and similarities which you value.
- You have an opportunity to learn to accept each other's differences and to become more tolerant.

Do you only see things from your own vantage point?

126

How to do the exercise:

1. Write down all your similarities and differences

You and your partner should do the first part of this exercise separately.

You should both now draw up 2 lists each:
- On one list, write down all the areas where you experience similarities between your partner and yourself.
- On the other list, write down all the areas where you experience differences between you.

2. Enjoy your similarities

Now sit down together and compare your lists of similarities. Notice the areas you have both included, find more similarities together, supplement each other's lists, and create an atmosphere of togetherness. Encourage each other and enjoy feeling good together.

This part of the exercise is extremely important in enabling you to discuss your differences later – without reacting negatively.

3. Explain and discuss your differences

Show each other your lists of differences – read them aloud to each other.

For each item or situation on your list, explain the attitudes, thoughts and feelings which underlie it.

4. Consider and classify your differences

Go through the lists of differences once more. Take one list at a time.

Indicate on your own list how you feel about each of the differences you have experienced. Let your partner do the same. Use the following criteria:

 I am happy about this difference. I want to encourage this behaviour. In other words: continue – let's have more of it. This difference is OK. You are OK.

 I have difficulty accepting this difference. You are OK, but I experience this behaviour as not-OK, and I would like you to change it if you want to.

 I do not have any strong feelings about this difference. I accept it and can live with it.

5. Make a contract

Discuss each other's assessments in detail.

Disregard the neutral assessments.

Both parties should accept the appreciation expressed in the other person's positive assessments.

Be open towards each other's negative assessments and perceive them as a challenge to improve.

Make a *contract* concerning your future behaviour and relationship.

Tell each other clearly:
- In which areas are you each prepared to follow the other person's desire for change?
- In which areas are each of you not prepared to change?
- In which areas are each of you willing to accept that the other person is not going to change – after having heard the reasons for his/her behaviour and attitudes?

Quality time

Your time is your life. Your life is made up of mornings, evenings, weekends, days off and work days. Your time can be well spent or wasted. Your time can be exciting or boring. Your time can be meaningful or meaningless.

You experience time in different ways depending upon what you are doing, who you are, and who you are with. Your perception of time also depends upon what has just happened in your life, where you are on your time continuum, and what you expect to experience in the future.

On the following pages, you can read about how a weekend can be ruined, or become a series of positive experiences – pearls.

You will also discover some exciting ways to look at time – which may become very important to you, both at work and at home. Finally, you will find some specific guidelines as to how you can create more quality time when you are with others.

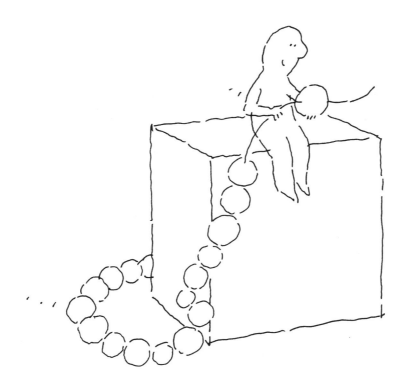

A bad weekend

How to ruin a winter weekend

I arrived home from work late one Friday evening and was looking forward to seeing my family. In the car on the way home, I had been thinking about my little son who would probably throw his arms around my neck when I walked in the door – and about my wonderful wife, who had probably got home from work before me, and would have prepared a nice dinner for us. I hate winter. I hate snow and sleet.

It would be wonderful to come home to my warm house, and to relax after the week's trials and tribulations with all those "foolish" people who were unable to comprehend the brilliance of my proposals.

On my way towards the front door, I stepped into a wet snowdrift and got snow in my shoes. I rang the doorbell, waited a little, and sure enough there they were – my wonderful little family. Peter threw his arms around me and said, "Daddy, Daddy, let's play Monopoly. Then we can all have fun." Alice smiled at me and asked sweetly, "Are you tired, sweetheart? Has it been a long day?" I gratefully recognised my wife's attempt to "save me" and tiredly nodded "yes" tiredly. Most of all I needed a drink and to relax a little.

*"Peter," I said, "come over here and sit in my chair and relax a little with me." Peter was delighted and was in fact prepared to sit quietly on my lap – for exactly 24 seconds. Then he got ants in his pants, and started to be a nuisance. "Daddy, can't we play a game or play with my cars?" Neither especially appealed to me; so under the pretence of having the whole weekend before us, I tricked him into going to bed – with a **very short** good night story instead of a long one. Alice came to my assistance with a goodnight song and an educational explanation to Peter about being tired when one has been working all day long. "Tomorrow, Daddy will play Monopoly with you, and maybe we can drive out to the woods and build a snowman." I nodded in agreement and turned off the light. Then to emphasise my agreement I repeated the word **maybe** twice. "Now let's have a nice, cozy evening together," Alice said, "I made a wonderful dinner. Why don't you find a nice bottle of red wine for us?"*

After two glasses of wine, the accumulated exhaustion of the week began to make itself felt, so I proposed that we moved into the living room and took our dessert and coffee by the television set. Alice agreed and, almost fully conscious and in what seemed to be a horizontal position, I enjoyed the first few scenes of a gangster film. It was about a bank robbery, I think. The leader of the gang had a scar above one eye. The police chief wore a beige cotton coat. Everything was planned down to the smallest detail... Then suddenly an alarm went off. It was very loud, and it kept on resounding in my ears. Suddenly Alice was in the film. She was standing next to me, shaking me. "It's time for bed," she said, "don't lie here sleeping in front of the TV." She turned it off, and the high-pitched, ear-splitting whine suddenly disappeared. I stumbled into the bedroom, and in the distance I heard Alice say something about brushing my teeth.

*The next morning I woke up suddenly. Something hard and square was being jabbed into my ribs. I threw back the blankets, and there was Peter with his Monopoly game. It was 6:30 a.m. Saturday morning. It was a northern winter – dark, cold and unpleasant outside. Alice turned over in the bed and whispered sweetly, "Play a game with him, or tell him a story here in bed. I'll fix some breakfast for us and bring it up." But I said, "Can't one even be allowed to sleep in peace when it's the weekend. Peter, go to your room and play for a bit. I'll give you 1£ for some sweets." When I woke up at 10 a.m., my head weighed a ton. Out in the kitchen, most of the breakfast had been cleared away, Alice was reading the newspaper, and Peter was drawing a picture. "This is for you, Daddy," he said with a big smile. "Shall I make some toast?" Alice asked. I mumbled something like I didn't think it was necessary. The bread had been on the table so long it was probably dry enough as it was! I always liked to be **funny** in the mornings.*

Alice served breakfast and sat down at the table with a quizzical look on her face, "What shall we do this weekend?" "I don't know," I said. "What's the weather forecast?" I didn't hear her answer.

I was reading the newspaper. Then Peter arrived and started pestering me again about playing Monopoly. "Can't you ever find anything to do by yourself?" I asked. "What about your friends?" "They aren't home," he answered. "Where's your mother?" I asked. Peter left the kitchen and came back a minute later and said, "Mummy is washing her hair."

Alice came out to the kitchen with wet hair. I suggested we take a drive and find some place nice where we could eat lunch. That didn't sound too exciting to Peter. He said all he wanted was a hot dog – and then sledging in the woods afterwards. Alice thought we should eat lunch at home and then go sledging. "Then we can have hot chocolate when we come home," she said. "Whoopee!" cried Peter.

I gave in.

"If you two drive over to the supermarket and bring home what's on my list, I'll set the table and dry my hair." I had to tell her I thought it would be easier if I went by myself. Getting Peter in and out of his snowsuit was no easy task, nor were his big laced winter boots. He started crying.

*"Okay," I said, "come along." But Peter was angry now and didn't want to go. **"You have to go,"** I said. Crying a little, he found his boots and snowsuit.*

After a long and difficult battle, I managed to get his feet into his boots and to lace them all the way up. That was when the frightened child meekly said, "Daddy, I can't put on my snowsuit when I've got my boots on."

Off came the boots. On went the snowsuit. Then on went the boots again, and the scarf, and the cap.

On the way out, Alice called, "Did he go to the loo?" No, he didn't go to the loo.

Into the hallway again. Scrape the snow off his boots. Into the bathroom. Off with all his clothes again. But Peter didn't have to go. It was when we were driving to the supermarket that he really had to go.

Out in the snow. The on-and-off ritual again. (Never eat yellow snow.)

There was a long, irritating queue at the supermarket. When I got home, Alice noticed that I had forgotten two of the items on her list, but she said, "We'll just have to eat our liver sausage without beetroots." (Personally, I think liver sausage without beetroots is rather unsophisticated. On the other hand, a beer or two at lunch is always nice.)

I insisted on taking a nap after lunch. Peter and Alice flatly refused. After a heated exchange, during which I explained the importance of my presence as a TV viewer to the afternoon's soccer match, Alice and Peter left on mission "Build-a-snowman".

I fell asleep in front of the television. The coloured pictures made falling asleep nice and easy.

I awoke to the sound of the key in the front door. "Mission snowman" was completed. Alice and Peter, their cheeks rosy, were the picture of health.

As compensation, I generously offered to participate in a game of Monopoly; but Peter didn't have the time. There was a children's programme he wanted to see on television, so he said, "We can play Monopoly afterwards." However, since I am not a believer in letting children have everything they want in life, I said to my son, "Peter, you must choose – the programme or Monopoly."

Alice had a vague, empty look on her face and she said, "Peter, I'll play Monopoly with you when the programme is over."

This of course delayed dinner. After Peter was put to bed, Alice reluctantly agreed to eat our late dinner in front of the television, so that we could (as I said), "make the most of our time". After dinner and the subsequent drink, Friday's ritual of falling asleep in front of the television repeated itself, only to be interrupted faithfully by that ear-splitting whine after the last programme.

Alice and I didn't sleep in each other's arms that night either...

The next morning, Peter started pestering me again with his Monopoly game... (children, fortunately, are equipped with indomitable optimism).

Do you recognise some, or all, of this weekend?

131

A good weekend

A dramatic change in our lives occurred when Alice suggested we work actively to plan better weekends. She proposed that every member of the family took a turn at being responsible for planning the "perfect weekend".

This was how her first proposal for a change in our winter weekends sounded:

"I suggest that you look after Peter as soon as you walk in the door Friday evening. Give him your full attention, and teach him something new in a fun and interesting way. Spend the time doing something you like so that Peter doesn't feel you are bored.

After a nice dinner, let's do something together. We could plan the best holiday ever, or make a list of all the people who are important to us and try to think of challenging, worthwhile and exciting ways to spend time with them – or we could invite our neighbours over for coffee and conversation.

Saturday morning we'll get up early.

You will go in and get Peter at 7 a.m. and snuggle up with him in our bed for half an hour while I take a shower. Then you and Peter can take a leisurely bath together.

Then both of you can go to the bakery and buy fresh bread while I set the table with candles and flowers.

We'll spend one whole hour eating breakfast together. Then while you clear the table and wash the dishes, I'll finish getting dressed.

After breakfast, we will take the train to the town and go our separate ways for a short while. You will take Peter to the Zoo and have ice cream at the café.

While you're doing that, I will go shopping. I might even stop by Anne's. She will definitely give me a cup of coffee.

At 1 p.m., we'll meet at our favourite restaurant, the old cellar place, for a nice lunch.

At 2 p.m., we'll go home again. Then you can watch the soccer on television while I take Peter to the cinema or go visit Grandmother.

I'll put an apple pie in the oven, so all you have to do is turn it on. If you want to invite Carl and his sons over to watch the game with you, you'll find the whipped cream in the refrigerator.

When Peter and I get home, the three of us can make dinner together.

After dinner, we'll put Peter to bed and you'll tell him a wonderful goodnight story – one you make up yourself. You enjoy letting your imagination run wild.

When Peter falls asleep, I'll put on that dress you like so much – and we'll let our imaginations run wild together.

Sunday we all went on a trip to the woods with our best friends.

It was absolutely the best weekend we have had in a long time.

Compare this weekend with the first.
It is the same family, the same main characters,
and the same number of hours. Families can decide
for themselves how they want to spend their time.
So can you.

**The more good weekends you create,
the better your life will be – it's all up to you.**

Psychological perceptions of time

The way people spend their time can be classified in different ways: working time and leisure time; time for serious activities and time for play; time spent maintaining the status quo and time spent developing something new, or time spent alone and time spent with others.

The degree of emotional involvement you feel when you are spending time with other people is vitally important to the quality of your time and your life.

Psychologists have divided the time we spend with other people into 6 main categories, each with a different degree of emotional involvement:

Isolation

Rituals

Pastimes

Activities

Games

Intimacy

On the following pages, typical behaviour and levels of involvement are described for each of these 6 ways of perceiving time.

Isolation

Isolation in the psychological sense describes a situation where you are with other people physically, but are isolated from them psychologically.

This does not mean things like isolating yourself physically by going for a walk alone, working alone or doing other things alone.

Isolation describes a state of mental passivity – i.e. when you chose not to communicate with the people around you.

Examples of isolation

Lifts
People often do not to speak to each other in lifts. They frequently avoid each other's eyes, look down or stare straight ahead. They don't say hello to each other. They act as though no one else is there, and they move to avoid body contact when a new person enters the lift.

Public Transport (aeroplanes/trains/buses)
In many countries, you can travel from one destination to another without exchanging a single word with the person sitting next to you.

Passengers often sit as far from each other as possible and if there is room, they try to block the seat next to them with their baggage. If someone dares take the seat, they look very offended.

Traffic
People usually ignore other drivers, and often there is a "free-for-all" atmosphere.

Lectures and meetings
When people attend courses, meetings or lectures with people they do not know, they often choose to isolate themselves. They do not speak to those around them, avoid their eyes, and study the list of participants on the table in front of them to find out who all the other strange people in the room are.

Oddly enough, some people even arrive early to make sure they can sit at the back of the room, in the worst possible seats, so they can leave easily – without attracting attention.

Accidental contacts
Many people do not speak to people they happen to meet in the hallway, at the reception desk, on the street, in the park, etc.

Rituals

Rituals can be described as stereotyped and predictable forms of behaviour – usually carried out on a superficial level.

The most common rituals are everyday hellos and goodbyes, such as this one:
"Good morning, Mrs. Jones."
"Good morning, Mr. Smith."
"How are you today?"
"I'm fine, thank you. How are you?"
"Oh quite well, thank you."

Other rituals are connected to mealtimes. In restaurants, the exchange between waiter and guest often sounds like this:
"I hope the food was satisfactory."
"Oh yes, it was quite delicious."
"I'm glad to hear you enjoyed it. Would you like some coffee?"
"No thank you. Let me have the bill please."
"Of course."

Wine tasting is another ritual at restaurants and hotels. Unfortunately, all the prescribed bowing often creates the opposite impression from the one desired.

Rituals are actions which everyone in a specific cultural group agrees should be carried out in more or less the same manner. They help make life feel orderly and secure; and negative reactions may result if the prevailing rituals are not respected.

In the right circumstances, rituals can also be entertaining and positive. Examples of this includes: awards ceremonies, greetings and congratulations, and toasting rituals.

Rituals also help people get to know one another and pave the way for deeper involvement.

When time spent with other people does not progress beyond the ritual stage, being together is rarely stimulating or inspiring – and no real "pearls" are created.

Pastimes

"Pastime" describes communication without much sign of interest from those involved.

Pastimes often naturally follow ritual greetings and entail slightly greater involvement.

At the pastime stage, people talk about innocuous subjects, skimming the surface, and "psyching" each other out. They ask each other questions without being especially interested in the answers.

Favorite topics are the weather, the political situation, food, cars, famous people, sports and other items which do not touch deeply upon the personal.

At the pastime stage, people exchange small strokes and pass the time without getting bored. Without getting too involved, people can get to know each other a little better and decide whether or not they want to become more deeply involved.

Examples of pastimes

While gardening, a neighbour calls over the fence to the neighbour next door:
"Your roses are really doing well."
"They should be at this time of the year."
"If the sun keeps shining like this, we certainly can't complain."

A passenger sits down next to the stewardess. After take-off, the passenger says:
"Do you fly a lot?"
"Oh yes, quite a lot."
"How long have you been a stewardess?"
"For about 3 years."
"It must be interesting to see so much of the world."
"It is; only we don't have much time when we are in other countries."
Then the stewardess says, as she gets up:
"Well, I guess I'd better get to work."
"Yes, there's plenty to look after."

A waiter says to a 5-year-old at his table: "What a big boy you are. Out for the day with Mum and Dad, are you?"
A negative response to a question like this would be a rare experience indeed!

A classic example of pastime behavior – old schoolmates bumping into each other on the street – is described on the next page.

Schoolmates

Two old schoolmates bump into each other accidentally on the street one day. Their conversation might well sound like this:

"It's been a long time."
"It certainly has."
"Tell me – what you are doing with yourself these days."
"Oh, I work for an insurance agency. What about you?"
"I'm at a computer company."
"Do you ever see any of the old crowd?"
"No, not much."
"Neither do I."
"Do you know what ever happened to Carl? Did he ever marry Mary?"
"No, I think I heard that Mary married a dentist from Liverpool."
"Just goes to show you. What about you? Are you married?"
"Oh yes, I got hooked, too."
"Do you have any children?"
"We have three – one 7, one 10 and one... about 14."
"So you have kids in every age group."
"Yes, I suppose you could say so. What about you? Do you have a family?"
"Yes, I have a wife and 2 children – one 7 and one only 2 years old."
"So there's a lot going on at home."
"There certainly is. Never a dull moment."
"Well, it was nice seeing you again."
"It certainly was."
"If you see any of the old crowd, give them my regards."
"I sure will, and I hope everything continues going well for you."
"Thank you. The best to you, too."
"Well, take care."
"Take care."

Activities

A more intense way of spending time with other people is to get involved in activities. At this stage, involvement is greater than at any of the 3 previously named stages.

At the activity stage, people do meaningful things together.

Most types of work done with other people can be regarded as activities, as can games and sports.

As a rule, activities represent useful, constructive, and inspiring ways of spending time together.

Examples of activities

- Neighbours help each other start a new lawnmower.

- Parents and children help each other wrap gifts.

- A group of employees work on a project together.

- Some friends go to the theatre together.

- The school orchestra plays together.

- A couple cooks dinner together.

- Students do homework together.

- Friends help move furniture into a new house.

At the activity stage, there is no "hidden agenda" between the people who are working together. Co-operation exists in an atmosphere of openness and mutual confidence. People help each other reach shared goals and enjoy being together while doing so.

Games

Unfortunately, people also engage in another type of activity – psychological games.

These games can take on the most fantastic forms; but common to them all is that there is no positive pay-off for participating in them or spending time on them.

At the games stage, it is difficult to see the connection between what people say and do, and what they really think and feel.

Games arise because of a deficit in people's stroke balance. People can actually fight for negative strokes because, in spite of everything, negative strokes are better than no strokes at all.

You have probably been involved in a number of games – both at home and at work.

Games are not rational; they are emotionally charged. The usual rules of common sense do not apply. It requires great psychological insight to understand that when people are upset about something, they have a tendency to take it out on others.

As mentioned earlier in this book, people are rarely angry for the reasons they give. Usually something else is bothering them – something which they may or may not be aware of. This "something" can trigger a psychological game.

The purpose of some games may be to communicate hidden, sarcastic, ironical or hostile messages to others. Other games may attempt to arouse pity and compassion in others (martyr games).

It is extremely beneficial to read more about psychological games – a subject dealt with in depth in other psychology books.

Try to identify which games you yourself play or are drawn into, and work actively to stop playing them.

Intimacy

People can also spend time together being intimate.

At this stage, the people who are involved all display an "I am OK – you are OK" attitude.

At intimate moments, people do not try to exploit each other. There are no false pretenses or defence mechanisms. People enjoy each other fully, give each other their complete attention, are genuinely considerate, and respect each other. An "invisible bubble" surrounds those involved.

Intimacy is the most sublime undertaking possible between human beings.

Examples of intimacy

- Being together and intensely enjoying music, a play, a trip, a discussion, a conversation, the countryside, or a culinary experience.

- Feeling genuine sympathy for other people's sorrow and joy

- Showing gratitude for another person's efforts

- Being together in connection with illness or death

- Saying goodbye to a close friend

- Being reunited with a close friend

- Enjoying intimate sexual relations

- Helping someone who really needs it in a genuine manner

Many forms of activity can be so intense that the borderline between activity and intimacy becomes unclear. For example, strong, intimate feelings can arise when a group of people are working intensely on a project together.

The only way to create quality time – pearls – in your life is to spend your time with others on activities and intimacy.

From isolation to intimacy

Maria attends a seminar

Maria attended a seminar in personal effectiveness. She was looking forward to the seminar which a good friend of hers recommended. Nevertheless, she was a little uncertain as to how it would feel to be with a group of people she did not know.

When she arrived at the conference centre, she followed the signs which led to the seminar hall. A hostess welcomed her, gave her the seminar material and a name tag, and pointed to the correct door. "You are welcome to sit wherever you like,", the hostess said. "It's best to sit as close to the front as possible."

Maria entered the half-filled lecture hall and looked for a place to sit. She chose a seat in the middle of the room, next to a friendly-looking woman in a red dress.

Isolation
Maria sat down next to the woman who was studying her seminar material. The woman's name tag read Gail Austin.

Maria also started studying her material. By looking at the list of participants, she discovered that Gail Austin worked in a bank, but it did not say what her position was.

Maria looked around the room, trying to get an idea of what the other people were like. Several new arrivals were also looking for a place to sit. Some of the participants were already sitting and talking to each other. Maria wondered if they knew each other, but she didn't say anything to Gail Austin since she didn't know her.

Then the programme began. Everyone listened attentively. It was exciting. A few times, Gail looked at Maria, but Maria quickly looked down at the material on the table in front of her.

Rituals
Shortly afterwards, the instructor began telling jokes. They were so funny that everyone roared with laughter. Maria laughed so hard tears ran down her cheeks. Gail laughed, too; and as if it was inevitable, Gail and Maria's eyes met during a burst of laughter.

When people finally stopped laughing, Maria caught Gail's eye again. Gail smiled. Now there was no going back. As if it was the most natural thing in the world, Gail gave Maria her hand. Maria took Gail's hand and said, "My name is Maria Thompson." "And mine is Gail Austin."

During the first break, Maria said, almost without thinking, "Well I can see you like going to seminars, too." "Yes," answered Gail, "you have to keep learning all the time."

Pastimes

Conversation between the two developed naturally during the coffee break:

"What kind of work do you do?"

"I work in a bank."

"Oh, that sounds exciting."

"Yes, it really is. There is so much new technology to learn about. What do you do?"

"I work at an advertising agency."

"There's a lot going on in advertising, too."

"There certainly is."

"Is anyone else from your agency here today?"

"Yes, two others, Leslie Jackson and Tom Peterson. They are both sitting in the first row, over by the window."

"It's a good idea when several people from the same company attend, because then they can discuss the programme together when it's over."

"You are quite right."

"Do you have any idea how long the lunch break is? I have to make a phone call."

"I would think it's an hour. But it must say so in the programme."

Activities

The conversation continued at lunch. Since Gail was standing behind her in the lunch queue, Maria gave her a plate. Maria liked Gail. She seemed self-confident, open and interested in other people. She also had some interesting opinions about things.

After lunch, there was group work. Gail and Maria were in the same group and helped each other to define their personal goals.

In the course of the next few breaks and group exercises, Maria became increasingly involved in discussion with Gail. The two women really started to get to know each other.

Intimacy

Unfortunately, their discussion was sharply interrupted during the afternoon coffee break on the second day of the seminar. There was a telephone call for Maria. Her son Johnny had had an accident while riding his bicycle and had been taken to hospital.

Maria left the conference centre in such a rush that she forgot to say goodbye to Gail. In all the commotion, she also forgot to take her seminar material with her.

Fortunately, her son was not badly hurt; and after a few stitches in the knee, a bandage and some ice cream, he was fine again.

An hour later, Maria and Johnny left the emergency room. Outside in the waiting room stood Gail. "I just wanted to know how your son was doing," she said with a smile. "He looks fine to me. And by the way Maria, I brought your seminar material along for you. I also took some notes for you, so you can get an idea of what you missed."

Time well-spent

The quality of your life will improve if you collect more pearls, in other words if you work systematically to spend less time on isolation, rituals, and pastimes and more time on meaningful activities and intimacy.

Moving from isolation to intimacy often occurs naturally while people go through the phases of trying to get to know each other. How fast you move from one level to the next depends on many things, e.g. your cultural background, your stroke balance, the situation, or the amount of openness and motivation you share with the other person.

You can work to shorten the process of moving from isolation to activities by being more open and involved.

You can also make an effort to spend more time on intimacy by learning to show your feelings, and being tolerant and interested in other people. By consciously spending your time on worthwhile activities, you will automatically experience more intimacy because some activities naturally lead to it.

How was your week?

Sit down in a comfortable chair and relax. Close your eyes. Think about what happened last week. Who were you with? What did you talk about? How did you spend your time?

Take one day at a time – then ask yourself the following questions for each day of the week:

- How much time did I spend with others on isolation?

- How much time did I spend with others on rituals?

- How much time did I spend with others on pastimes?

- How much time did I spend with others on activities?

- How much time did I spend with others on games?

- How much time did I spend with others on intimacy?

Use the chart to assess how satisfied you are with the past week. Place your ×s on the chart using the following guidelines:

5: Highly satisfactory. A real pearl – with lots of activities and intimacy. I will remember this day with real pleasure.

4: A good day. I am satisfied with it. I used a lot of my time on activities and also experienced some intimacy.

3: Nothing to complain about. The day was like so many others. Nothing exceptional happened. A greater part of the day was taken up by pastimes and routines. There was also time for a few activities, but there was no real intimacy.

2: Unsatisfactory. A sad and meaningless day. I didn't achieve anything other than pastimes. A day I am not proud of.

1: A really bad day. A completely meaningless day. I wasted my time on isolation and/or games. Pearls were crushed. A day I would prefer to forget.

My assessment / Days of the week	5	4	3	2	1
Monday					
Tuesday					
Wednesday					
Thursday					
Friday					
Saturday					
Sunday					

Was the past week typical for you?

Did you spend enough time on activities and intimacy?

Reflect about time every once in a while!

Avoid isolation – you can just as easily say hello to people, even people you do not know.
Once you have reached the ritual stage, conversation is not so far away.

Become more involved in communicating with other people.
Turn pastimes into activities.

Spend as much time as possible on activities and intimacy.
Then there will be less space between the pearls on your string.
In this way, you improve the quality of your time and your life.

Variety in life

Everyone needs both security and challenges.

Every time you remain within ordinary limits and do things the way you are used to doing them, you experience a feeling of security. When conditions around you are orderly, predictable and coincide with your expectations, you can relax and feel safe. Family traditions and ordinary, everyday habits and routines help you live your life without too much pressure and strain.

In order for people to function well, it is necessary to experience a certain amount of security and predictability. But if there are too few challenges, there is also a chance that life will become too predictable, boring and unexciting.

To experience challenges, you must ensure that life includes variety, surprises and unpredictable moments.

When it comes to living harmoniously, the amount of security and variety people need varies from person to person, and everyone must find their own balance between the two.

In relationships between men and women, it is important that both are aware of their own need for variety and challenge as well as the needs of the other person. Many couples break up because they become inactive and lose the ability to renew themselves. They become unable to inspire and challenge each other. In other cases, the needs of partners for variety and challenge are simply not the same.

Variety means change. Change means development.

Variety can help make your life more exciting. You are more inspiring to be with, and utilise your creative talents more fully.

Variety can help you find new ways to do things – and to see solutions you were unable to see previously.

By always sticking to what is safe and what you know, you limit your development and lose the ability to inspire others.

Do you look for new challenges? Or do you stick to what you know?

Is there variety in your life? Or do people always know where they are with you?

Are you an exciting person to be around?

Is your repertoire of behavioural modes large enough?

Do you have several different ways of solving problems?

Make sure your life does not become too routine.

Meet new people. Do new things.

Be creative – concoct news ways of bringing variety into your life.

Every time you try something new and succeed, your self-esteem is strengthened, which is why you should actively seek to create variety.

Try to develop your ability to change, vary and modify yourself. Don't stop your development...

Examples of ingrained habits

Drinking habits

Many people ask for the same drink every time they are offered one. Eventually, this becomes so well-known that the host automatically pours for his guests and says, "Whiskey on the rocks for John, dry vermouth for Anne, orange juice for Peter, a cold beer for Curt, and a gin and tonic for Ruth." Deeply impressed, the guests ask, "How can you remember what we all drink?" And the host answers, "Now that I've known you for 20 years, the least I can do is know what you drink."

Are you one of those people who have fixed drinking habits?

Why not try a new drink the next time you are asked? For the sake of variety, if nothing else. When the host asks, "What will it be?" you could answer, "What do you have?" If you are offered something you have never tried before, give it a try. You might even like it. In any case, you will surprise your friends.

Eating habits

Some people have learned to live with a limited repertoire of dishes. It is easy and convenient and makes no great demands on their imagination or creativity. Likewise, many people have a tendency to choose the same dishes almost every time they go out to eat.

Are your eating habits too ingrained?

What about adding something you have never tried before to the week's regular repertoire of dishes? Why not introduce a culinary theme of the week, an Italian week, a French week, or a vegetarian week?

Families can create variety by letting each member take a turn being responsible for selecting the menu and for doing the shopping and the cooking.

Next time you are at a restaurant, why not let the waiter or the chef select the dinner for you? You might also try different restaurants.

Jump out of your habits.

The dinner party

Dinner parties often goes like this:

The guests arrive with a bottle of wine and a small gift for the host and hostess, either flowers or chocolates. The hostess then says what she is supposed to say, "Oh you shouldn't have, it's far too much."

The guests are then offered a welcome drink, "Whisky on the rocks for John, dry vermouth for Anne..."

Then it is time to go to the dinner table. The appetizer, either smoked salmon or a shrimp cocktail, is already on the table, and is accompanied by a glass of white wine.

Then the main dish arrives: sirloin steak with a salad and french bread. Red wine is served. This course is followed by a little cheese and the remainder of the red wine. After the cheese comes dessert.

Then, of course, the stage is set for the evening's big surprise.

The host says, "I have an idea!"

The guests, who are full of expectation, look at each other, "I wonder what's up now?"

The host continues, "Why don't we..."

The tension rises to the boiling point. The guests are thinking, "What now? What now?"

The host says, "Why don't we take our coffee in the living room?"

Everyone agrees to this "daring" proposal and moves to the living room, complimenting the dinner as they go.

Cognac and liqueur are served with the coffee, after which there are goodnight drinks, "Whisky on the rocks for John, dry vermouth for Anne..."

Finally, there are the touching goodbyes. Everyone agrees it has been a wonderful evening, and that the food was delicious. The guests leave with full stomachs, and plenty of ideas for arranging a dinner party themselves – one where there will be absolutely no chance of going beyond the bounds of convention.

How conventional are you, when you give a party?

The parties you and your guests remember best are probably the ones which stand out because they were different.

You can vary your social gatherings by arranging an unexpected welcoming ceremony, by writing a song, starting a contest, taking part in some unconventional activities, eating and drinking something new and different, serving dishes in different ways, involving your guests in the preparations, changing the dress rules, varying the guest list, or choosing another time to start or finish.

There are lots of possibilities for variety. Discover more yourself.

When you are the guest, try to think about varying the gifts you take: there is more to life than flowers, chocolate and wine.

Travelling to and from work

Many people choose the same type of transport and the same route to and from work every day. For some, driving home from work is so deeply ingrained that they can do the whole journey without even thinking about it. Suddenly they are parked in front of their own house, quite horrified, thinking, "How in the world did I get here? I hope I didn't go through too many red lights!"

Do you recognise this situation?

What about choosing another route home once in a while? It might give you a new perspective on life. Be sure to make your travel entertaining and useful – by enjoying some good music, or listening to a course on tape.

Holidays

Quite a few people choose to spend their holidays at the same place every year, i.e. at their cottage. Seeing the place again is wonderful, especially when the whole family is once more sitting on the veranda, looking out over the fields rippling in the wind – just like last year... and the year before.

Do you vary your holidays?

Why not sell the cottage? Or at least try a completely new kind of holiday every other year?

"The home-coming ritual"

Upon arriving home, the husband or wife says, "How often do I have to tell you I don't want to see Johnny's dirty rubber boots out here in the hall?"

The partner replies dryly, "I can hear you are home."

What about changing your home-coming ritual? What about saying something like, "I have just had this splendid idea. Why don't we open a shop for rubber boots?" When your partner answers, "We probably don't have enough boots," you could answer, "Oh I don't know about that. Every time I come home, I find a pair in the hall."

EXERCISE 16: More variety in my life

Create variety in your life by varying your drinking habits, eating habits, behaviour, use of time, holidays, ways of travelling, social gatherings, circle of friends, methods of dealing with problems and tasks, etc.

List below what you plan to do in order to create more excitement and challenges in your life.

Areas in which I want to create variety	I plan to do/try the following	By when	√

Stress management

Everyone has an idea of what the word stress means, but most people find it difficult to define the concept clearly.

When you say, "I feel stressed," you are probably feeling tired, irritated, exhausted, depressed, tense and disappointed.

Normally, people look upon stress as something negative.

Stress can be a negative thing; but it is also essential for our survival. Stress is always with us, and we all need a certain amount of it in order to function properly. However, both too little and too much stress can cause problems.

It is not a question of avoiding stress, but rather of learning to manage it, and to utilise it positively.

Advantages of being able to manage stress:

- You avoid unnecessary "wear and tear" on your body.
- You improve your physical and psychological well-being.
- You solve problems faster and more effectively.
- You get along better with others.

What is stress?

People are continually exposed to a variety of influences to which they react.

Each of these is registered in your brain as a demand, a change or a strain – i.e. a *stressor*.

Stress can be defined as:

The way your body reacts when you are exposed to stressors.

In order to manage your stress and make the best possible use of it, you must be aware of:

- What happens to you mentally and physically when you are exposed to stressors
- Which stressors affect you most
- Which signals tell you that you are under stress
- Which methods can you use to manage your stress better and to make the most of it

The stress response

When you are exposed to stress, you react with the stress response.

In some cases, this response leads to exhaustion, irritation, frustration and illness. In other cases, the stress response may be crucial in determining whether you can cope with a situation and perhaps even survive.

When the brain registers a stressor, it immediately determines what response is demanded. Is this a purely routine situation, or does it in fact represent a threat or an exciting challenge? This assessment determines the strength and duration of the response.

The stress response consists of the following:

- More adrenaline is secreted
- Breathing becomes more rapid
- Blood pressure rises
- Muscle tension increases
- Senses are sharpened
- Immune system functions are reduced

In order for the stress response to lead to positive and suitable action, it must be appropriate, both in terms of strength and duration, to the demands of the actual stressor.

The stress response triggers the mobilisation of energy which normally consists of 3 phases:

1. *Alarm and mobilisation phase:* The body is activated and energy is mobilised.
2. *Adaptation phase:* The alarm phase reaction lessens and the level of energy adjusts to the demands.
3. *Return phase:* The energy level returns to normal.

The effects of stress

Stress can affect you negatively or positively, depending on how you experience a situation.

Negative effects

The negative effects of stress are generated if too much or too little energy is mobilised in response, or if the stressor is not removed, or if you do not have the opportunity to act.

These effects show themselves particularly in your state of health, in the level of your performance, and in your behaviour. Some appear immediately, while others first surface after a long period of high level of stress.

Positive effects

The positive effects of stress emerge when the amount of energy that is mobilised is appropriate to the stressor. Or when the stressor is removed and the energy is used and not allowed to accumulate, or when you are able to act.

The stress response puts you into a state of readiness and increases your chances of preventing threats and heading off attacks.

In the right amounts, stress has a stimulating effect. Most people thrive when they are faced with a certain number of demands and challenges.

Stress enables you to mobilise all your forces in particularly demanding situations: sports contests, examinations, etc.

When you succeed in adapting your stress response to the stressor, you will experience stress energy as an extra strength which adds spice to your life.

If you learn to manage your stress, you can lengthen your life and improve its quality.

My stressors

In order to manage your stress, it is important to find out what causes it, i.e. what *your stressors* are.
Stressors can be divided into two main groups:

Tangible stressors

Stressors which are tangible, easy to ascertain and describe, and which originate in the technical, economic, physical or professional world:

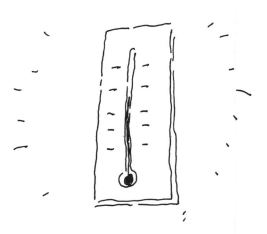

- heat
- cold
- noise
- traffic
- health
- tools
- pollution
- disorder
- housing conditions
- accommodation at work/home
- lighting
- waiting time
- finances
- taxes
- quality demands
- deadlines
- interruptions
- workload
- lack of information
- etc.

Emotional stressors

Stressors which are intangible and emotional, and which originate in the world of human relationships, attitudes, perceptions and behaviour:

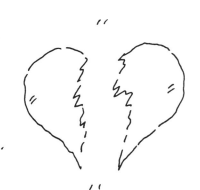

- disappointments
- differences in values/norms
- matters of conscience
- power struggles
- chicanery
- problems in co-operating
- difficulties in communicating
- jealousy
- breaches of contract/agreements
- inability to act
- etc.

What makes you feel stressed? Can you identify your stressors?

EXERCISE 17: My stressors

List below the stressors which influence you negatively – both at home and at work.

For each stressor, indicate what you plan to do about it: 1) remove it, 2) reduce its negative effect, or 3) learn to live with it.

My stressors	What I plan to do		
	Remove	Reduce	Live with it

You can only do something about your stressors when you know what they are.
By being aware of them, you have already solved an important part of your problems.
Discuss your stressors with the people you live and work with.
Learn also to identify their negative stressors.

My stress signals

Everyone has their own unique stress threshold which sets the limits for how much strain the body can cope with. When you go beyond this threshold, your body reacts by sending out *stress signals:* symptoms of your body being overtaxed.

Stress signals appear as a kind of red light, or warning signal, to remind you to do something. The longer you wait before reacting to these signals, the greater the chance of damaging your body, and the more difficult it will become to mend the damage.

These signals are symptoms telling you that something is wrong. They are sending you an important message: Be careful! Take it easy!

Stress signals can be divided into general and specific signals.

General signals

When the stress response leads to greater mobilisation of energy, the following general signals occur in everyone:

- Breathing becomes more rapid
- Muscles are tensed

These signals are a part of the normal stress process. They occur both when stress is experienced as something positive or as something negative – and are not necessarily a sign of danger.

Specific signals

Everyone has their own stress signals. They can be physical or psychological in nature. They can appear immediately or after a while:

- muscle tension
- headaches
- digestive problems
- allergies
- fatigue
- decreased ability to concentrate
- aggression
- reduced tolerance
- nervousness
- changes in patterns of eating and drinking
- changes in smoking habits
- etc.

Learn to notice your stress signals. Even if you have never thought about them before, they are there.

What stress signals do you experience?

156

EXERCISE 18: My stress signals

List below your stress signals and the situations in which you experience them. Let the examples on the preceding page inspire you, or ask the people who know you well to tell you which signals they notice.

My stress signals	Situations they occur in

Choose the signals you experience most often, and learn to pay attention to them.

Only by being aware of your stress signals, can you do something about them. First of all, you can find out what caused the signal, and secondly, you can act upon that cause.

Remember it is important to cure the cause of the stress signal, not the symptom itself. An ulcer should be treated before it arises, i.e. at the first sign of acid regurgitation.

Discuss your stress signals with the people you live and work with; and learn to identify the stress signals of others.

Methods for managing stress

You have now gained a greater awareness of both your stressors and your stress signals, and you know something about the positive and negative effects of stress.

Being aware of what stress means to you enables you to learn to manage your stress more effectively.

By managing your stress you can achieve:

- better health
- a longer life
- an enhanced quality of life

Consciously or unconsciously, everyone uses some form of stress management to cope with tense situations in the short term.

Some people console themselves by eating, others chain smoke or consume more coffee or alcohol. Others take hot baths, go jogging in the woods, or let off steam by shouting.

On the following pages, you will find inspiration and methods for managing your stress.

Two types of approach are necessary for stress management:

Here-and-now methods

to quickly reduce your present level of stress

Long-term methods

to gradually build up your resistance to stress and to raise your stress threshold

Here-and-now methods

A here-and-now method brings speedy relief by reducing your present level of stress immediately. Here-and-now methods are directed towards the two general stress signals which warn that, here and now, your level of stress is becoming too high:

– Your breathing is more rapid than normal

– Your muscles are more tense than normal

Here-and-now methods are particularly effective in the short term. They are not directed towards the cause of stress but only towards the symptoms.

Regulating your breathing

Breathing is the most important key to quickly reducing your stress level. The rate of respiration, which indicates the degree of tension, is easy to observe and to correct immediately.

When breathing is calm, it is impossible to maintain a high level of tension.

If you can maintain your normal rate of respiration while in a stressful situation, your stress level will fall and be easier to manage.

What to do
Make a habit of controlling your breathing several times a day.

Follow the guidelines on the next page

Work consciously to regulate your breathing whenever the rate of respiration is more rapid than normal. For example:

● Whenever you notice your breathing has become too rapid.

● Whenever you have to make a special efforts: athletic contests, lectures, speeches, examinations, etc.

● Whenever you are in a situation which could easily provoke aggravation, irritation, frustration, disappointment, aggression, etc.

● Whenever you have time to spare: waiting, travelling, during breaks, etc.

● Whenever your activities make it possible: while doing routine work, watching television, listening to music, taking a bath, etc.

You can reduce your present level of stress by using the method for regulating your breathing described on page 160. It will also affect your performance and your sense of well-being right here and now.

This method is not only suitable for immediate relief of stress. It can also have a positive long-term effect.

If, for example, you do the exercise regularly, three times a day, you will continually interrupt, and therefore reduce, the accumulation of stress which inevitably takes place. As a result, you will be able to cope with more stress, and you will have more energy.

EXERCISE 19: Regulating my breathing

1. Sit back comfortably in a chair so that your body is well supported and does not slump – or lie down on a bed or on the floor. If you cannot sit or lie down, you can do this exercise standing.

2. Make sure your clothing in not too tight.

3. Take a deep breath – and breathe out slowly.

4. Breathe in and out normally.

5. Continue breathing normally, and at the same time notice how your stomach expands and contracts as you breathe in and out.

   Feel the rhythm:

   – Stomach expands
   – Stomach contracts

   – Stomach expands
   – Stomach contracts

6. When you feel your breathing is calm, start saying to yourself:

   As you breathe in – "I am..."
   As you breathe out – "...relaxed."

7. Continue the exercise until you feel you are comfortably relaxed and ready to deal with the task facing you - or continue for as long as the time allows.

Relaxing your muscles

Tense muscles, like rapid breathing, are a symptom which is easy to do something about.

The muscular tension that builds up in your body during the day is not caused by stress alone. Much of it is due to bad habits.

What kind of habits do you have? Do you sit correctly? Are your desk and chair the right height? Do you hold your telephone and writing instruments correctly? Do you walk properly? Do you have good posture? Are your movements appropriate to the tasks you do? Do you avoid straining your body?

Whether muscular tension is caused by stress or bad habits, it will eventually lead to a higher level of stress if you do not do something about it.

What to do
Several times a day, pay attention to your muscles. Are they tense or relaxed? Notice if you are doing anything which causes unnecessary muscular tension.

On the next page, you will find here-and-now methods for relaxing your muscles.

Use these methods in the following situations:

- Whenever you notice stiffness or tension in your muscles.

- Whenever you have been in the same position for a long time.

- Whenever you have been lifting or carrying something heavy.

- Whenever you have been performing the same movements repeatedly, for a long time.

- Whenever you have extra time: waiting, travelling, during breaks, etc.

- Whenever your activities make it possible: while sitting in your car, watching television, listening to music, taking a bath, etc.

If used regularly – and not just when stress signals occur – these methods for relaxing muscular tension will also have a long-term effect on your well-being.

Make it a habit to cultivate activities which relax your muscles. This will help reduce the accumulation of stress. As a result, you will be able to cope with more stress, and you will have more energy.

Methods for relaxing your muscles

There are many methods for rapid relief of muscular tension. Choose a method you like and which feels natural to you. For example:

- Stretch – carefully – as far as you can
- Shake your arms and legs
- Dance
- Yawn vigorously
- Tense the muscles in your arms and legs – then relax them
- Sing or whistle
- Take a hot bath
- Take a sauna
- Make a funny face – hold it tight – and then relax
- Laugh
- Exercise
- Get a massage

Relaxing your neck and shoulder muscles
The neck and shoulders are particularly prone to muscular tension.

It is vital to your well-being that you reduce these tensions.

What to do
1. Sit down or stand so that your neck and shoulder muscles can move freely.

2. Use the method for regulating your breathing which was described earlier, until your breathing is calm.

3. Draw the numbers 1, 2, 3, 4, 5, 6, 7, 8, 9, 0 in the air with your nose. Draw them big and move slowly. Take a break between each number.

4. Concentrate on your movements and feel how the muscles in your neck and shoulders become loose.

Long-term methods

The purpose of using long-term methods of stress management is to strengthen yourself so that your physical and mental resistance increases. As a result, your stress threshold increases. You become better at managing your stress response and at using positively the energy created.

The long-term methods affect your lifestyle. Long-term stress management is synonymous with a change of habit.

In the short term, it is useful to clear your desk when you start to lose overview. In the long term, it is a matter of establishing working habits which ensure that mountains of paperwork never accumulate on your desk.

In the short term, you benefit from a good night's sleep when you have had a tough schedule for some time. In the long term, you should develop good sleeping habits so you do not tire so easily.

When you practice long-term methods of stress management, you stay healthy, prolong your life, and enjoy life.

Long-term methods help you create healthy lifestyle habits within the following areas:

- Sleep
- Rest
- Exercise
- Nutrition
- Relaxation
- Overview and control

Sleep

Simply being awake exposes your body to wear and tear. Your cells are broken down more rapidly than you can regenerate them.

When you are awake, your body secretes various hormones which have a stimulating effect and which increase your capacity and ability to react. At the same time, these hormones inhibit the regeneration of cells.

The production of hormones which inhibit cell regeneration slows down almost completely when you sleep. Instead, other hormones are produced which strengthen your muscles and promote cell growth.

When you sleep deeply and adequately, you are rested and restored when you wake up.

The cycle of sleep

If you get to know your sleep cycle – follow it reasonably well – the quality of your sleep will improve greatly.

Pay attention to the body signals which indicate that it is time to sleep, e.g. sitting and nodding off in front of the television set. Go to bed instead of forcing yourself to stay awake.

Do not go to bed early unless you are tired. People need different amounts of sleep. The amount of sleep you need will also vary from time to time, and usually, decreases with age. Sleeping for eight hours is often more than a person needs.

When should you get up?

It is important for your level of energy and well-being that you get up at the right time.

Preferably, it should be at a point in your sleep cycle when you are sleeping lightly. If you are sleeping deeply when you awaken, you will feel lousy and get off to a bad start that day.

Set your alarm to go off at least 15 minutes before you have to get up, so your body has time to wake up slowly.

Rest

As well as sleep, the body also needs short periods of rest and has a natural daily rhythm which alternates between activity and rest. This need for rest occurs about every second hour and manifests itself as a loss of concentration, slight lethargy, or the need for a cup of coffee.

Coffee will stimulate you immediately, but this is not what your body is asking for. It is asking for a rest, and the best course of action would be to give it just that. Find a way to relax for a few moments. You will then feel refreshed and be able to work and concentrate better than before.

Exercise

Nature intended human beings to be physically active: but modern lifestyles are such that many people are far too inactive physically in their daily life. Organs and muscles weaken if they are not used sufficiently which is why we need to exercise.

Exercise trains and strengthens the heart, lungs and muscles, and helps you discharge the body's waste products. Exercise is "active relaxation" which means that you can, in fact, walk or run yourself out of tiredness or tension.

Accustom yourself to some form of regular exercise. The easiest form is a brisk walk everyday, or a daily bicycle ride, e.g. to and from work.

If you cannot include some form of regular exercise in your daily activities, think of some you can pursue in your leisure time.

Choose something you like, and do it regularly.

Nutrition

You are what you eat!

Your body needs protein, carbohydrates and fats, as well as vitamins, minerals and trace elements. These substances provide for the renewal of worn tissue and enable the organs to function properly.

Animals have a natural instinct for what is healthy for them and how much they should eat.

If people had this instinct at one time, it has long since been lost.

There is not enough variety in the diet of many people, and some eat either too little or too much.

There are many good reasons for paying attention to how and what you eat; as the cause of much illness is "right on your plate".

Proper nutrition is "insurance" against many types of illness – and it is important for your well-being, your appearance and your emotional stability.

Proper nutrition is a great step forward – towards "the good life". Nutritional experts can help you find the "right" diet.

Relaxation

Just as the body needs physical exercise, it also needs relaxation.

Relaxation techniques reduce both psychological and physical tension.

You need to acquire the habit of regularly allowing your body a period of deep relaxation. This demands training, patience and a continuous effort.

For instance, you can get a massage, practice yoga or other relaxation exercises, or you can learn relaxation techniques from books or tapes.

Find the type of relaxation which suits you best.

Overview and control

One of the main causes of stress is the uncertainty which arises from lack of overview.

You can gain more control over your life and lessen the amount of the stress you experience by learning to plan and create results. Try to keep the next 24 hours constantly under control as described in chapter 1.

Positive thinking

Your attitude to yourself and your surroundings largely determines whether or not you succeed in controlling stress. You will be more successful if you think positively.

The expectations you have concerning future events largely determine whether or not these events are experienced as positive or negative, stressful or challenging.

This happens because the image you have of the coming event influences your feelings and your body. Whether you are looking forward to something, or are apprehensive about it, your mind and body are part of the situation. Your expectation as to what is going to happen can also influence what actually does happen.

Positive thinking has nothing to do with unrealistic optimism. Positive thinking is a form of mental discipline.

For example, sportsmen and women, who must perform under great pressure, spend a great deal of time preparing themselves mentally.

Most people agree that you get more out of thinking positively than thinking negatively. Nevertheless, the actions of many people are an expression of negative thinking.

Positive people often use the word "so", while negative people often use the word "but".

Here are some examples of statements made by people with a *"but" attitude:*

- I would like to put forward more ideas here at work, *but* my boss would probably not have time to listen to them.

- I would have gone for a walk, *but* it was raining; so I stayed in.

- I would like to recommend the best solution to my customers, *but* they will just think I am trying to pull a fast one on them.

- I can see a lot of things here at the office which could be improved at very little cost, *but* it will only be regarded as criticism if I put forward my ideas.

Think how much more could be gained by having a *"so" attitude:*

- I would like to put forward more ideas here at work, but my boss is busy; *so* I will have to choose a good time to present them.

- I wanted to go for a walk but it was raining; *so* I put on my raincoat and went for a wonderful walk in the rain.

- I would like to recommend the best solution to my customers; *so* I must find a way of presenting it which does not seem pushy.

- I can see a lot of things here at the office which could be improved at very little cost; *so* I must find a way of suggesting things without my colleagues feeling that it is some kind of criticism.

My goodness, how expensive everything is!

It has become quite a sport, especially in the prosperous welfare societies of Northern Europe, to pass the time making imaginative pronouncements about the evils of the rising cost of living.

Many after-dinner conversations go like this:

Aunt Alma leads the overture of grievances for the evening:

"Yesterday I was at the supermarket and bought some coffee, a bottle of wine, 2 jars of marmalade, 12 eggs and a packet of corn flakes. And do you know how much it cost?..." "No," *reply the rest of the happy musicians,* "how much did it cost?" "18,75," *sounds Aunt Alma's fiddle, followed by the whole orchestra...* "My goodness, how expensive everything is!"

How interesting this evening could have been if the discussion had touched upon a positive and worthwhile topic.

We brood and fret because what costs 10£ today once cost only 1£. Even though we actually have more 10£ notes in our pockets today than we once had 1£ notes, professional brooders still prefer to say, "That's not the way to look at things if one wants to brood and fret."

Far too many people worry about things they cannot change. We fret about the rising cost of oil, instead of learning to live with it. We discuss how much tax we have to pay instead of how much money we have *at our disposal.*

Many people live so well that they really have to be creative to find something in their lives to criticise. We forget the important things in life. Small grievances get blown up. We lose our sense of proportion.

People who are healthy forget to appreciate their good health and spend far too much time being annoyed because their train is five minutes late, or because there is too little salad dressing, or because the waiter is inattentive, or because it is raining when they hoped for sunshine.

Negative thought patterns like this only darken your existence.

Make a decision right now! Choose to think positively. Enjoy the things you have. Enjoy the things you can do.

It should not be necessary for you to lose your health or mobility to discover how important being healthy and being able to move about freely really are.

Live while you have got life to live.

Negative thoughts

Another type of negative thinking which people frequently indulge in is anticipating problems before they actually occur. Such people experience all the pain and sorrow before anything bad takes place.

For instance, if the boss is sitting in a meeting behind closed doors, you often hear someone in the outer office comment, "They are probably sitting in there talking about us. We'll probably all get fired."

When a company introduces a new system, many employees choose to regard it as a control measure rather than as a useful aid to help secure jobs.

When a new colleague puts forward suggestions for improvement, senior people often concentrate on the right of this new employee with "limited experience" to come in and try making changes, rather than on the suggestions themselves.

Think how much more they could gain from having the attitude: Here comes a new colleague with fresh ideas and opinions which could certainly help us renew ourselves.

It is often the "take care" people who are fond of enjoying misfortune in advance – both for themselves and others. "Take care you don't trip and fall." "Take care you don't drop the baby... or get robbed, mugged, have an accident... etc."

One of the most negative attitudes is envy.

Instead of working for their own success, some people work for other people's failure.

Stop envying others. Be pleased with their success and ask them for good advice so that you can succeed in your own field.

Positive thinking is an expression of the joy of living.
Negative thinking expresses sorrow for what is not.

You can learn to see the positive in every situation:

- Focus on the cheese – not on the holes in it.

- Be happy for the money you have at your disposal – do not fret about taxation.

- If you feel that other people are more successful than you are, invest time in learning what it would take for you to reach that level. Do not waste time pulling other people down to your level – you can spend your whole life trying.

- Look upon every problem as a challenge.

Stop fretting and worrying
There are only 2 kinds of problems:

- The ones you can do something about
- The ones you can do nothing about

It does not pay to worry about either of them.
There is no reason to worry about the problems you can do something about – just do something about them.
There is no reason to worry about the problems you can do nothing about – because you can do nothing about them anyway!

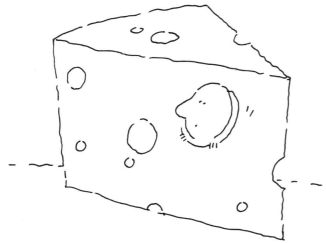

Enjoy life – in spite of everything,
it may just be better than the alternative.

Make stress management a habit

Stress management is an important habit which demands time, motivation and a certain amount of self-discipline to learn.

If you make the long-term methods a permanent part of your lifestyle, you will experience a number of positive effects. You gain more control over things, save time and energy, and avoid feeling driven and bad tempered. You become more resistant to life's demands and strains; you generate more time, and feel more like enjoying life.

If you try to incorporate all the long-term methods for stress management into your life at a single sweep, they may seem overwhelming and very time-consuming. It is better to take one area at a time, starting with the one you think is most important for you.

You can choose a relaxed or a more disciplined attitude towards stress management. Do not be afraid to experiment and make changes as you discover new possibilities.

In a short time, stress management will be a natural and indispensable part of your life.

Rapport and pacing

Everyone recognises two lovers sitting together in a restaurant.

They look deep into each other's eyes, and each mirrors the way the other sits. Their heads tilt in the same direction, and they lift their wine glasses in exactly the same way at exactly the same time. These two people are *pacing* each other.

Studies show that in situations like this, lovers do more than just reflect each other's body language.

They speak in the same tone of voice, at the same speed, using the same words, jargon, idioms and phrases. They also breathe at the same rate.

They are in *rapport* with each other.

What is rapport?

Rapport exists between people when there is a mutual feeling of harmony and well-being, which could also be described as sympathy or *resonance*. Resonance is the phenomenon that occurs when you strike a note with one tuning fork and hold it close to a second, which then begins to vibrate in harmony.

A pure, noble and intense resonance occurs between people when they live and work together in an atmosphere of openness and trust.

Rapport means that a relationship is close, trusting, open, free, safe and comfortable.

It means meeting people at their own level, where they feel safe and at home; and it is characterised by harmony, mutual respect and a feeling of belonging.

Rapport exists when people like each other and are on the same wavelength.

In other words, you are in rapport to the extent that your words, body language/tone of voice or other similarities harmonise or "swing" with those of another person.

You can regard people from two completely different standpoints:

1. You can choose to focus on *the differences* between you,

   or

2. You can choose to focus on *the similarities* – the things you agree about, feel the same about, or react to in the same way.

You will find it almost impossible to create rapport with another person if you emphasise the differences between you. But by concentrating on what you have in common, you will discover that resistance, conflicts of interest, mistrust, scepticism, fear, anger and other inappropriate and damaging feelings disappear more easily.

People really do have a lot in common. With a little practice, it is not difficult to find the similarities in others and to feel sympathy for them.

When people identify with each other, they are better able to work and live together, more willing to listen to criticism, more open to new ideas and changes, and prepared to give of themselves – to make an extra effort.

When people are in rapport, they *pace* each other *unconsciously*.

Rapport is the noblest way people can relate to each other.

What is pacing?

Pacing can be defined as any type of "mirroring" by one person of another. It is the best way to create rapport.

Pacing is the process which takes place when you meet someone else in his/her world by reflecting the other person's body language, tone of voice, choice of words and feelings – so that they feel your behaviour blends harmoniously with their own.

Pacing means showing the other person those aspects of yourself which are closest to their nature and attitudes.

We all have a tendency to like people who are similar to us, and we want to be in complete agreement with these people.

We communicate best with people we feel are like us. And who see the world as we see it, and have similar preferences.

We choose our friends among the people who make us feel good.

Pacing or "mirroring" happens quite *unconsciously* when there is empathy between people – in other words when they are in rapport.

Lack of rapport can occur because people don't know each other, or would rather wait and see, or are feeling reserved, sceptical, nervous, frustrated, defensive, aggressive, or find themselves in a situation which is discordant in some way. In cases like this, pacing can be used *consciously* to achieve rapport.

An important goal for any kind of communication is to achieve and maintain rapport. The best way to achieve rapport is pacing.

Pacing

You can pace other people in many ways. Here is a list of examples of ways in which you can do this:

Body language
- Sitting position
- Position of legs
- Posture
- Position of head
- Arm movements
- Manner of walking
- Dress
- Facial expressions
- Breathing
- Degree and manner of touching

Speech
- Tone of voice
- Speed and strength of voice
- Choice of words
- Intonation
- Jargon
- Use of foreign words and technical terms

Attitudes/feelings/moods
- Attitudes
- Opinions
- Commitment
- Tolerance
- Sorrow
- Happiness
- Anger
- Enthusiasm

Pacing allows you to identify more easily with the conscious or unconscious feelings of other people, and thus understand them better.

You can greatly improve your relations with someone by merely adjusting your tone of voice and the speed at which you speak so that you harmonise with them.

Many conflicts arise because one person speaks very rapidly and the other very slowly. This irritates the fasttalker, who then speaks even more quickly; this causes the person who speaks slowly to feel insecure and frustrated and react by speaking even more slowly.

It is easy for people who are highly knowledgeable in their field to unconsciously intimidate others by speaking too rapidly, or by using many technical terms.

For example, this can be particularly unpleasant in the doctor/patient interaction. Many patients feel uncomfortable and uninformed in the presence of doctors who "dispace" them by brushing aside questions quickly, not looking at them, and generally paying them very little attention.

The doctor's behaviour probably reveals a very realistic picture of his or her thoughts, i.e: "It's time to finish, there are other patients waiting" or "I am the expert, I know all the answers".

Pacing employees

By pacing employees who have new ideas, a manager can increase their level of performance and their desire to present more ideas.

Example:
A manager is sitting at the desk writing a letter. An enthusiastic employee comes through the door and says, "Good morning! Listen to this! I've got a marvellous idea!"

The manager does not answer, stays seated at the desk, doesn't look up, continues writing and then, after a short pause, and still without looking up, says: "An idea? What kind of an idea?... Can't it wait?"

This type of dispacing takes place every day all around the world and has a very negative effect on co-operation and effectiveness.

A true *improvement* could have been achieved if the manager had got up immediately when the employee entered, and said, "Good morning," and then listened to the idea while mirroring the employee's posture. Then the manager could have put a hand on the employee's shoulder and said, "That sounds exciting. Right now I have to finish this. Then, let's have a cup of coffee in the conference room, say, in an hour. Will you make sure we are not interrupted... I'll see you at 11... and by the way, thanks for sharing your ideas with me."

Pacing children

You can also improve relationships with your children by pacing them when they come to you.

An example:
As soon as his father walks through the door after a long day at work, his little son says, "Daddy, let's play draughts." And his mother adds, "You promised."

The father answers in a voice full of irritation, with his shoulder turned towards his son – and without bending forward or looking at his child, "OK, OK. Go get the board." (Between the lines, his body language is saying: "... let's get it over with.")

Grandparents seldom act like this towards their grandchildren.

If a grandfather receives the same proposal, he will probably display more physical and mental closeness. He will turn directly towards the child, bend down on one knee to be at the same height, and say with a smile in his eyes, "OK, you little rascal, go get the board... what colour do you want?" Thus he will create rapport with his grandchild.

We know there is a direct link between what goes on in one's mind and what the body shows.

The father demonstrated clearly with his body that he didn't feel like playing draughts right then and there. While the grandfather's body language also clearly reflected his thoughts: "I just adore this kid. Isn't it wonderful that my grandchildren feel like spending time with me." As well as, "I guess I spent far too little time with my own children."

EXERCISE 20: My personal pacing programme

Rapport is the goal – pacing is the means.
Work consciously to create better rapport: get to know your own "natural pace".

A. Get to know your natural pace

Indicate your natural pace by placing ✕s in the boxes below. You can also indicate the pace of other people on this chart by marking their characteristics with different colours. In this way, you can gain an overview of how easily harmony or disharmony arises between yourself and others.

Speech/auditive expression

Rate	low ＿＿＿ high	Vocal pitch	low ＿＿＿ high
Sentence length	long ＿＿＿ short	Clichés	many ＿＿＿ few
Jargon	much ＿＿＿ little	Vocal strength	low ＿＿＿ high
Technical terms foreign words	many ＿＿＿ few	Imagery	little ＿＿＿ much

Body language/visual expression

Gestures	few ＿＿＿ many	Facial expression	neutral ＿＿＿ lively
Eye contact	little ＿＿＿ much	Dress	informal ＿＿＿ formal
Touching others	little ＿＿＿ much	Colour choice (e.g. clothes)	discreet ＿＿＿ crude
Movements	slow ＿＿＿ rapid	Status symbols	few ＿＿＿ many

Other signals

Tolerance level	low ＿＿＿ high	Mode of expression	visual ＿＿＿ auditive
Enthusiasm	little ＿＿＿ much	Manner	reserved ＿＿＿ candid
Sympathetic	little ＿＿＿ much	Preferred style of communication	written ＿＿＿ spoken
Intuition	weak ＿＿＿ strong	Humour	little ＿＿＿ much

B. Distinguishing characteristics of your own pace

Form a picture of your natural pace by looking at all your responses in section A of this exercise. Describe briefly your distinguishing characteristics, e.g. "I speak quickly, etc."

You might even ask someone who knows you well to evaluate your assessment of your own pace. Do you agree with each other?

Pay special attention when you are with people whose pace deviates noticeably from yours in terms of these characteristics.

C. Positive experiences

Describe some situations where you experienced intense rapport/harmony with others:

Why did things go so well? What can you do to create the same situation again?

to be continued

D. Negative experiences

Describe some situations where you experienced intense disharmony with others:

Do you often experience disharmony with others? What goes wrong?

What can you do to avoid disharmony? What *will* you do?

E. Greater tolerance

List some persons who are difficult for you to accept and describe why:

Who?   Why?

What can you do to become more tolerant of these people? What *will* you do?

7 sensible guidelines for achieving rapport

1. Know your own natural pace
2. Be aware of the pace of others
3. Be tolerant of people's differences
4. Learn to concentrate on the similarities you share
5. Do not criticise or reprimand others before you have achieved rapport
6. Try to position yourself so that pacing comes easily and naturally
7. Be particularly careful to pace people during the first 4 minutes you are with them

Your time and your life become more worthwhile every time you achieve rapport with another person.

EXERCISE 21: Creating rapport

Describe below what you can do to build better relations with the world around you by using pacing.

In what specific areas do you think you can improve?

Should you pay particular attention to your body, feelings/moods or voice? In which situations should you be particularly careful? Describe situations from home and work.

At work	At home

Put out your antennae every time you are with another person. Pace that person!

Continually analyse positive and negative experiences. Learn from them!

In the future, be aware of situations where you feel uncomfortable or experience uneasiness. Notice the things in the non-verbal communication of both yourself and others which may be causing the problem.

Make it a habit to work consciously to create rapport – when you do, you are opening the door to a new and exciting world.

A positive alternative

A way of creating rapport is "A positive alternative".
Here are some examples of how a situation can
develop in completely different directions, depending
on how it is tackled.

How I dispaced my family

One evening my wife came home late. She asked
me to make dinner and have it ready by 9 o'clock.
She said our 5-year-old son could help me cook,
but that I should be careful he didn't burn his fingers when I was doing the steaks.

My son was playing with his cars on the floor in
the living room; so I tiptoed out to the kitchen
without saying a word to him and began making
dinner.

A minute later he was standing by my side,
pulling at my trousers and saying proudly, "Daddy,
I'll help you do the steaks." I said, "No son, you
know you're too little for that, and Mummy says
you might burn your fingers..."

Since my son is as stubborn as his parents, he
didn't give up so easily. "Daddy, I *want to* help you
with the steaks. Why can't I?" At the same time,
he reached for the carving fork. "Didn't I say you
might burn yourself? Are you listening to me?"
And I slapped his fingers. He began to cry and ran
out of the kitchen. He kicked his cars and ran into
his room, slamming the door.

A minute later my wife arrived. She understood
the situation immediately and said, "What's happened? Where's Peter?"

"In his room," I said. "He got angry because
he wasn't allowed to cook the steaks. That just
goes to show you what happens if you are firm
with kids..."

A long quarrel followed. It ended with me acting
the martyr, and refusing to eat dinner with them.

How I could create rapport

In the previous situation, it might have been better
to use the "positive alternative" technique. Just
think if the conversation had gone like this:

Peter: "Daddy, can I help you with the steaks?"

Father (as he bends over): "Oh, do you really
want to help me cook?" (The father paces and creates rapport.)

Peter: "I sure do!"

Father: "That's just great. Go and get an
apron." (So the father has a moment to think of
a good, positive alternative.) "Can you make
the salad? Or are you too small?"

Peter: "Of course I can make the salad."

Father: "Well then, let me see you do it."

A minute later, Peter is in full flow next to his
father, rinsing and drying the lettuce, while his
father is doing the steaks.

Father: "Quiet! Who do you think is coming
now? Did you hear the key in the door? It's
Mummy. Run and tell her not to come out into
the dining room. We have a little surprise for
her."

A minute later, Peter calls his mother.
"Mummy, time for dinner." The kitchen crew
marches into the dining room, which is decorated with candles and flowers. Peter brings in
the salad. His father brings in the steaks.

Father: "Mother, can you guess who made the
salad?"

Peter (with big eyes): "Mummy I did!"

It doesn't demand much imagination to picture
how "A positive alternative" can save an evening.

The first 4 minutes

The first contact between people can lead to harmony or disharmony, enjoyment or frustration, security or insecurity, openness or reluctance, love or hate.

That first contact – *the first 4 minutes* – determines how the relationship will develop.

Sympathy or antipathy is largely determined by the way in which two people communicate during those first 4 minutes, using words, tone of voice, and body language.

If rapport is not achieved during the first 4 minutes, it will negatively affect the subsequent communication.

Why the first 4 minutes?

This is no arbitrary amount of time. By observing people in different contact situations, scientists have discovered that it takes, on the average, about 4 minutes for people to decide if the contact between them should continue or if they should part.

During the first 4 minutes, it also becomes clear whether rapport is going to be created or not. When two people start talking, they are almost "forced" to continue talking to each other for about 4 minutes before it feels "natural" to end the conversation.

You have probably had the experience of meeting someone and immediately feeling that you were both on the same wavelength – or of meeting someone and everything went wrong right from the start.

Be aware of the importance of the first 4 minutes – this short, introductory period determines whether you will form a positive relationship or not.

By pacing during the first 4 minutes, you can create rapport and develop a relationship. If you dispace, you are almost sure to create disharmony.

Normally, it is wise to pay special attention to the first 4 minutes in the following 4 situations:

- When you come home in the evening
- When you wake up in the morning
- When you arrive at work
- When you meet someone new

In the evening

Many people wade in through the door in the evening after work without ever giving a thought to what they should say in order to create a positive atmosphere around them – and to create the foundation for a good, active evening.

The first 4 minutes are often spent on rituals and pastimes, talking about the traffic, the weather, or the day's chores. Often clichés like these are heard:

"Were you a good boy in school today?"
"How was your day?"
"When do we eat?"
"Is there anything good on TV tonight?"
"Did anyone call?"
"Did anyone walk the dog?"
"Who took the newspaper?"

The first 4 minutes can also be used to communicate opinions such as:

"Do your shoes always have to be in the hallway?"
"Couldn't you have wiped your feet before you came in?"
"Close the door behind you, it's cold."
"Did you call the plumber?"
"There wasn't any petrol in the car this morning, so it was your fault that I was almost late for work."
"When you use my car, couldn't you at least empty the ashtray when you are finished?"

If you want to make sure your evenings are worthwhile, think for a minute before you walk through the door.

Vary your behaviour when you get home so you don't fall into using the same routine homecoming ritual everyday.

Prepare what you are going to say. Think about the strokes you could give. Remember the importance of your body language. Have some ideas ready to make the evening exciting.

If you live alone, it is also important that you do something positive with the first 4 minutes when you arrive home in the evening. Play some music. Be good to yourself. Put on some comfortable clothes. Set the table nicely. You deserve good food. Spoil yourself a little.

James Bond
- and the first 4 minutes

Have you ever seen a James Bond movie?

Perhaps 007 was "working" under water – in the Bosporus – in his diving suit. He has been fighting with 170 of Doctor No's frogmen, and was bitten in the rear by a huge shark filled with atomic weapons.

But James Bond never complains when he comes home from work. He has mastered the first 4 minutes.

When he gets back to "Sylvia Bond", he peels off his wet suit – and lo and behold! – what does he have underneath? You guessed it – his white tuxedo.

Then he says with a charming smile, "Good evening. My name is Bond.... James Bond!"

Why not try coming home one evening like James Bond and saying, "Good evening. My name is Adams... George Adams!" But don't forget to take off your wet suit!

In the morning

For many couples, the first few minutes in the morning have over the years become a boring, ritualistic and uninspiring process which affects the whole morning and even the desire to get up. This time is crucial to how you feel when you go to work, and affects your mood throughout the day.

Over the year, some spouses – especially husbands – have developed an unpleasant morning habit. They "pass wind" on their way from the bed to the bathroom.

Don't do it! There are so many other ways of expressing yourself, or creating an atmosphere...

When the alarm clock rings, many start complaining to their husbands or wives:

"Boy am I sleepy!"

"It can't be 7 o'clock already!"

A positive alternative

When the alarm clock goes off, your body language can demonstrate that you still have an appetite for life. If your partner says, "Stop it, stop it! We'll be late for work," you can display your foresight, "No we won't! I set the alarm an hour early!"

If you want to be certain that your mornings are worthwhile, think about the first 4 minutes.

Try to vary the start of the day. Be loving and kind to your partner and your children. Think positively and talk about something positive. Set the alarm an hour earlier every once in awhile, and try to find a creative way of using the extra time.

Make sure you have enough time to enjoy your mornings and avoid rushing.

At work

Very often, meeting your boss, colleagues and employees on a daily basis, can seem like an insignificant and boring routine.

Why not give your day a flying start?

Give strokes to the people you meet.

Find something new to say.

Notice the changes in your surroundings, and let people know you have noticed them.

New people

Pay extra attention during the first 4 minutes when you meet someone new.

Use your antennae. Catch all signals.

Pay attention to the other person's body language, tone of voice and choice of words.

Meet them in their world.

Remember that non-verbal communication is the most important. Even if you only have a few seconds, you can still make eye contact, smile and pace.

Remember too that a smile to your local merchants, local authority workers, cleaning personnel, traffic wardens and people you meet in traffic can work wonders.

If you pay attention to your behaviour during the first 4 minutes, you will be able to greatly improve your relationships.

The last  minutes

When you are with others,
think about "the last 4 minutes" too
– every time you are about to leave a situation.

The last impression people get of you
has great significance for your relations
with them and determines whether or not
they will be looking forward
to the next "first 4 minutes" with you.

8. I own the problem

After reading this book and doing the exercises, you are now equipped with many ideas and strategies which can help you continue your development.

You have probably recognised many of the examples in this book and have a lot to think about.

Maybe some of the proposals were new to you, while others were not – and some were obvious.

It is more than likely that you feel inspired to make some changes in yourself and to learn something new.

While continuing your personal development, it is very helpful to have the attitude that "I own the problem".

This book is about you and your development – not about other people and their development.

For instance, don't say to your husband or wife, "You should read this book. You could really learn something from it – and so could your brother." This probably won't inspire your partner to read it.

Do not be disappointed if others do not share your enthusiasm – especially if your "new" bright idea seems pretty obvious, or is something they thought you should have done a long time ago, anyway.

For example, if you say to your husband/wife:

"I just read a great book. Now listen to this. We should spend more time with the children. We should remember each other's birthdays. We should be more active in our leisure time, and should read between the lines. We should be more tolerant, and shouldn't get upset over unimportant things. We should also create variety in our lives."

– your partner might just make the following comment:

"I sure hope you didn't buy that book. There's nothing in it that I haven't been telling you for years now. But you never listen to me."

If your husband or wife reacts like this, you might be tempted to think, "The problem at our house is you and your attitude."

This is a totally erroneous way of looking at the problem.

I own the problem.

The problem is that I am not good enough at inspiring my partner; or I haven't found the right time and the right way to present my ideas.

Every time you point an accusing finger at someone else – to indicate who is the cause of a problem and the source of all the world's misfortune and misery – try to remember that only one finger is pointing towards the other person.

Three fingers are pointing back at yourself...

There is probably a good reason for this.

Don't talk so much about what you want to do. Do it instead! As you develop and carry out some of your resolutions, other people will notice and may even feel like following you.

When your husband or wife says: "What a wonderful time we had. What's happened to you?"

– you might casually say:

"Oh, not much. I just read a book on personal development. It helped me understand some of my faults and weaknesses. I am trying to work on them now."

When your partner then says:

"It really seems to have worked. I would like to see that book. Couldn't we talk about it together? I have so many faults and weaknesses I would like to work on, too."

– you might reply:

"Why should you change, my friend? I like you just the way you are."

The last remark will probably really stimulate your partner's interest in the book.

Actually, it's not a bad idea to discuss your time and your life with the people who share it.

Do not feel that you are a victim of circumstance.
Understand that you "own" the problems
– and you are the only one who can solve them.

Don't think and say:

"Unfortunately, I must
leave the meeting now."

"My boss interrupts me
all the time."

"I am late because of
the weather."

"I don't have time to
learn a new language
because of all the chores
I have at home."

"You talk so much that
I can't get a word in."

Think and say instead:

"I have not allowed
enough time."

"I let myself
be interrupted."

"I left home late."

"I didn't give languages a
sufficiently high priority."

"I am unable to get
your attention."

I choose my own life!

*If your life is worthwhile,
it is your own doing – it is not just luck.*

*If your life is not worthwhile,
it is also your own doing – and not just bad luck.*

You must learn to understand that you are choosing the life you live.

You are responsible for your actions and your behaviour. You alone decide how you are going to deal with the situation you are in right now. You alone can change your life.

Not before you realise this can you take control of your own life. Taking control determines whether or not you will be able to enjoy life fully and feel free.

Learn to see your life as the result of a series of decisions – choices – you have made.

Do not look upon your life as the result of other people's decisions and choices.

When you say: "I don't have any choice," you are fooling yourself. What you really mean is that you do not like the choices, and that instead of trying to influence them, you accept the choices others have made for you.

To go along "of your own free will" is also a choice. Your choice. And it is a bad choice.

Every time you do something which goes against your deepest beliefs, you will have less self-esteem. This will lead to feelings of guilt, frustration, lack of commitment, and inadequacy.

You will not only feel better about yourself if you realise that the choice is yours, you will also feel better when you are with other people.

Since you are the one who has to live with your choices – for the rest of your life – it is important to make decisions you can live with.

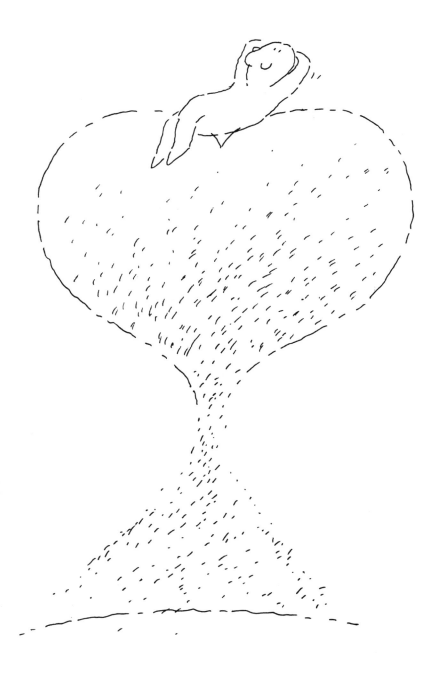

Book list

Personal development and attitudes towards life

Bach, Richard:
Jonathan Livingstone Seagull.
Pan Books. London 1973. ISBN 0-330-23647-4.

Bono, Edward de:
Lateral Thinking.
Harper & Row. New York 1990. ISBN 0-06-090325-2.

Dyer, Wayne W.:
The Sky's the Limit.
Pocket Books. New York 1984. ISBN 0-671-24989-4.

Dyer, Wayne W.:
Your Erroneous Zones.
Avon. New York 1977. ISBN 0-380-01669-9.

Fulghum, Robert:
All I Really Need to Know I Learned in Kindergarten.
Villard Books. New York 1989. ISBN 0-394-57102-9.

Hoff, Benjamin:
The Tao of Pooh.
Penguin Books. New York 1983. ISBN 0-14-006747-7 Pbk.

Pirsig, Robert M.:
Zen and the Art of Motorcycle Maintenance.
William Morrow. New York 1974. ISBN 0-688-00230-7.

Russell, Peter:
The Brain Book.
Know Your Own Mind and How to Use It.
Routledge & Kegan Paul Ltd. London/Henley-on-Thames 1982.
ISBN 0-7100-0706-X Pbk.

Saint-Exupery, Antoine de:
The Little Prince.
Harecourt Brace Jovanovich. San Diego 1982. ISBN 0-15-646511-6 Pbk.

Strokes

Berne, Eric:
Games People Play.
Ballantine Books. New York 1985. ISBN 0-345-32719 Pbk.

Harris, Thomas A. & Amy Bjork Harris:
Staying OK.
Harper & Row. New York 1985. ISBN 0-06-015311-6.

Harris, Thomas A.:
I'm OK - You're OK.
Pan Books. London 1973. ISBN 0-330-23543-5.

James, M. & D. Jongeward:
Born to Win.
Addison-Wesley. Reading 1971. ISBN 0-201-03319-4 Pbk.

Stress-management

Fontana, David:
Managing Stress.
British Psychological Society/Routledge. London 1989.
ISBN 0-901715-97-2 Pbk.

Madders, Jane:
Stress and Relaxation.
Arco Publications Co. New York 1979. ISBN 0-668-04674-0.

Selye, Hans:
Stress Without Distress.
NAL. 1975. ISBN 0-451-16192-0.

Rapport and pacing

Argyle, Michael:
Bodily Communication.
Routledge. London 1990. ISBN 0-415-05114-2.

Richardson, J. & J. Margulis:
The Magic of Rapport.
Harbor Publishing. San Francisco 1981. ISBN 0-936602-26-6.

Zunin, L. & N.:
Contact - The First Four Minutes.
Ballantine Books. New York 1980. ISBN 0-345-28662-6.

"Living in the moment", page 17, and "More haste", page 110, is reprinted with the permission of Piet Hein A/S, Denmark.

TMI publications

TMI publishes books and other publications to help individuals, teams and organisations achieve results. The publications are used as participants' materials on TMI programmes, but are also suitable for self-tuition. Some of the publications are international "best-sellers".

All publications are written in a style which combines carefully prepared educational principles with a number of startling ideas and concepts taken from our recognisable day-to-day life – both at home and at work. The publications are packed with concentrated know-how. They are based on all accessible literature and on TMI's experience, gained through more than 20 years, of helping people and organisations in all parts of the world grow and develop.

The publications are different from and more than just books. They are written seminars with an inspirational part and an implementation part. The subject matter is easily accessible and practically applicable with many illustrations, exercises, tests, checklists and other tools to put the recommendations into practice.

Every TMI publication is aimed at everybody in all businesses in the private as well as the public sector – irrespective of profession.

Something about gold-searchers

People and organisations need the right information in order to be able to grow and develop. The search for the right information and the ability to transform it to applicable knowledge can be compared to searching for gold. Just like the gold is hidden in masses of sand and deep down in the ground, vital knowledge is mostly hidden in a mass of unnecessary information. Only a few have the resources and time for this gold-searchers work.

TMI has established a development team of specialists who work as professional gold-searchers.

They have developed advanced methods of:

– finding the places where the gold is to be found.
– extracting the gold and washing away the sand.
– presenting the gold so it is not just decorative, but practically applicable.
– transforming information to knowledge of lasting value.

All publications can be ordered direct from TMI.

TMI books

Employeeship
Mobilising everyone's energy to win.
A unique TMI concept, which helps people in organisations develop a special, personal commitment to the success of the company.
A TMI book illustrating what it takes to be a good employee, and how the energy of all employees can be mobilised to ensure the survival and growth of the company.

The book provides inspiration and methods for everyone to show responsibility, loyalty and initiative. The book also gives specific suggestions for the policies and systems the company should adopt and implement to bring out the best in everyone.
ISBN 87-89264-97-5.
TMI order number 4007.

My Life Tree
A different book about personal development.
"My Life Tree" is about what the individual – as a staff member or a manager – can do to achieve continuous, positive development and growth.

The book provides inspiration and practical help to develop a positive attitude towards life, create good relations towards others, define and achieve personal goals and acquire knowledge and skills.
ISBN 87-89264-70-3.
TMI order number 4006.

Personal Quality
The basis of all other quality.
The TMI quality concept focuses on the human side of quality.
The book contains a large number of concrete methods, checklists and exercises to help you develop your own personal quality and the departmental quality.

The concept is heralded as *"no less than a breakthrough within quality development"* by the British Department of Trade and Industry and the European Organisation for Quality.
ISBN 87-88036-73-1.
TMI order number 4021.

Putting People First
Personal service through personal development.
An international best-seller.
Both a tool and a source of inspiration for people who would like to get more out of their lives as service-providers. The book gives advice in how to perceive and meet customer expectations, how to handle stressful situations, how to interpret other people's body language and how to use one's own body language to achieve harmony and a great deal more.

The book teaches you what it takes to provide good professional service and feel good about yourself and the people around you, both at home and at work.
ISBN 87-89937-23-6.
TMI order number 4000.

TMI booklets
"Building bricks"

*TMI's booklets are modules of knowledge – bricks to build up
the exact combination of knowledge which you and your organisation needs.*

A Complaint is a Gift
From complaint to satisfaction.
**A TMI tool to help you regain your unhappy
customers' trust and keep your customers.**
This booklet is a practical tool for employees with customer contact, and for those responsible for developing an organisation's complaints policy.
ISBN 87-89937-03-1.
TMI order number 4309.

Be a Double Bagger
*Bringing out the best in yourself and in others
– at home and at work.*
**A TMI tool to strengthen your self-esteem and
encourage others.**
Be a Double Bagger is about personal development, which is a prerequisite to the development of the organisation. An organisation's ability to attract and keep capable employees and thus create an environment in which everybody wishes to do their best is determined by the degree with which the organisation stakes on the development of the individual person.
   The publication contains an inspirational part and a tool part.
ISBN 87-89937-26-0.
TMI order number 4314.

Delegation
*Delegate, have confidence in others
and increase their competence.*
A TMI tool to develop the delegation skill of management and the competence of staff.
Effective delegation implies that the manager assigns power and authority to staff and that staff are willing and able to take responsibility. The booklet outlines the "hard" and "soft" rules which management and staff need to adhere to in order to make the delegation process work.
ISBN 87-88036-52-9.
TMI order number 4022.

Energy Meter
Is everyone's energy mobilised towards winning?
3 TMI tools to measure and improve an organisation's potential to survive and develop:
1. **The Personal Employeeship Meter.**
   Is the person a good employee: responsible, loyal and full of initative?
2. **The Departmental Employeeship Meter.**
   Is everybody committed to the survival and development of the organisation?
3. **The Organisational Employeeship Meter**
   Does the organisation's culture, systems and policies inspire the employees to do their best?
ISBN 87-89264-96-7.
TMI order number 4307.

Personal Guarantee
Associate your name with quality.
**A TMI tool to anticipate and prevent errors, and
win other people's trust.**
The object of implementing Personal Guarantee is to improve the quality of every single detail in every action performed by every employee in the organisation.
ISBN 87-89937-02-3.
TMI order number 4308.

Personal Organisation
*Overview, order, system and control
– at home and at work.*
**A TMI tool to create overview, increase your level
of performance and improve your personal productivity.**
"Personal Organisation" is a practical workbook, packed with techniques, instructions, check-lists, ideas and inspiration for efficient personal organisation at work and at home.
ISBN 87-89264-26-6.
TMI order number 4014.

Reaching for the Stars
A book about team quality
A TMI tool to develop top quality in all teams and ensure the success of the organisation.
This book is about the special kind of quality which is performed in a team and which is vital to the total quality of the organisation.

The book contains tools to monitor and develop the quality of a team's total performance as well as the quality climate of the team.

The book is for top managers, team managers and employees in the private and public sector.
ISBN 87-89937-22-8.
TMI order number 4310.

Time Manager
The key to personal effectiveness.
A self-instructional guide in the use of the Time Manager.
This user guide is in itself a complete, concise training course in personal effectiveness. The guide contains much good advice on how to define your goals and create a link between your goals, tasks and the use of your time as well as how to adapt the Time Manager tool to your own needs.
ISBN 87-89264-81-9.
TMI order number 4041.

How to contact

TMI Head Office
Time Manager International A/S · Huginsvej 8 · DK-3400 Hillerød · Denmark
Telephone: +45 42 26 26 88 · Telefax: +45 42 26 54 55 · Telex: 42118 tmint dk

Telephone, fax or write to us if you would like information about TMI's products and seminars, or if you would like to receive the latest list of the names and addresses of TMI's representatives in more than 35 countries:

Australia	Greenland	Middle East	Sweden
Austria	Hong Kong	Netherlands	Switzerland
Belgium	Hungary	New Zealand	Taiwan
Cyprus	Iceland	Norway	Thailand
Czech Republic	India	Philippines	Turkey
Finland	Ireland	Portugal	Ukraine
France	Italy	Russia	United Kingdom
Germany	Japan	Singapore	USA
Greece	Mexico	Spain	

Australia
TMI Australia
45 Chandos Street
P.O. Box 263
Crows Nest 2065
Telephone: +61 2 439 6844
Telefax: +61 2 436 2091

Belgium
TMI Belgium
1, Rue Général de Gaulle
B-1310 La Hulpe
Telephone: +32 2 653 8830
Telefax: +32 2 653 9397

Cyprus and Middle East
IPA Systems Consultants Ltd.
44-46 Acropolis Avenue
P.O. Box 8693
Acropolis,
Nicosia, Cyprus
Telephone: +357 2 494718
Telefax: +357 2 494451

Hong Kong
TMI Hong Kong
3701 Wu Chung House
213 Queen's Road East
Hong Kong
Telephone: +852 2893 2228
Telefax: +852 2893 7504

India
GSI Training
and Development Pvt. Ltd.
C-72, Neeti Bagh
New Delhi - 110049
Telephone: +91 11 6866657
Telefax: +91 11 6854667

Ireland
TMI Training Consultants Ltd.
2 Clonskeagh Square
Clonskeagh
Dublin 14
Telephone: +353 1 283 0925
Telefax: +353 1 269 7816

México
TMI México
Zimat Servicios Plus, SA de CV
Río Churubusco 422
(Coyoacán)
México, D.F. 04100
México
Telephone + 525 659 1631/5163
Telefax: + 525 554 7075

New Zealand
TMI Pacific Ltd.
9 Hardley Ave., Tindalls Bay
P.O.Box 136
Whangaparaoa 1463, HBC
Telephone: +64 9 424 7243
Telefax: +64 9 424 7245

Philippines
TMI Philippines
Unit D 1 Garden Level
Corinthian Plaza
121 Paseo de Roxas, Makati
Metro Manila
Telephone: +632 813 2968
Telefax: +632 813 4927

Singapore
TMI Singapore
Times Conferences Pte. Ltd.
1 New Industrial Road
4th Floor, Times Centre
Singapore 1953
Telephone: +65 284 8844
Telefax: +65 286 5754

Taiwan
TMI Taiwan
6th Floor No. 184
Fu Shing N. Road
Taipei, Taiwan, R.O.C.
Telephone: +886 2 515 2888
Telefax: +886 2 515 2889

Thailand
TMI Thailand
PNS Management Co. Ltd.
16th Floor
Lake Rajada Office Complex
193/64 Ratchadapisek Road
Khlong Toey, Bangkok 101 10
Telephone: +662 264 0457/0458
Telefax: +662 264 0459

United Kingdom
TMI United Kingdom
50 High Street
Henley-in-Arden, Solihull
West Midlands B95 5AN
Telephone: +44 1564 794100
Telefax: +44 1564 793033

USA
TMI North America Inc.
33 New Montgomery Street
Suite 310
San Francisco, CA 94105
Telephone: +1 415 957 1133
Telefax: +1 415 882 4960